EXPLO[illegible]
LOCAL HISTORY

a Practical Guide for Teachers in Primary and Secondary Schools

Geoff Timmins

School of Humanities and Social Sciences
University of Central Lancashire

Exploring Local History: a Practical Guide for Teachers in Primary and Secondary Schools

Published by the British Association for Local History 2018

Typeset in ITC New Baskerville by John Chandler
Printed by Lightning Source

ISBN 978-0-948140-03-7

Front cover illustration
This carefully-posed photograph was taken on the last day tolls were levied on Preston New Road, which runs between Blackburn and Preston in Lancashire. It shows Shackerley toll house at Mellor, near Blackburn. The windows in the projecting, angled frontage of the house enabled the toll keeper to view the road in either direction. The toll board, which listed the charges for different types of traffic, was situated above the front door at a convenient height for those travelling on horseback or on horse-drawn vehicles. A lamp was provided so that the charges could be seen at night. The porch gave some shelter when tolls were being collected. Two rooms in the house could be heated – there were two chimney pots and hence two flues leading to fireplaces – but it is not clear how many rooms there were altogether. Rainwater was collected in a barrel for domestic use. The milestone gives the distance to Preston as seven miles. The photograph probably dates from the late 1880s.

Contents

Acknowledgements

I would like to thank members of the British Association for Local History's Outreach and Publications Advisory Committees for the encouragement and advice they have offered in preparing this guide. In particular, I am much indebted to Tim Lomas for reading and commenting constructively on an earlier draft of the script and to John Chandler and Paul Carter for their design inputs. I am also greatly indebted to Carol Timmins, who has provided invaluable help in preparing the script for publication. I have been able to draw on a highly stimulating selection of works dealing with learning and teaching approaches in local history, especially the articles written by teachers that appear in the Historical Association's *Teaching History* and *Primary History* journals. These contributions testify to the important role that studying local history can have in promoting children's learning. Any errors are my responsibility.

Introduction

This guide has two main aims. The first is to address key considerations that arise in teaching local history at primary and secondary levels, bearing in mind the requirements made by the National Curriculum and the GCSE awarding bodies. The second is to consider examples of local history exercises that can be undertaken by primary and secondary school children, drawing on the types of documentary and non-documentary source material that are available in most localities and that are relatively easy to access. The emphasis is on devising active learning approaches that involve children in guided investigations designed to further their historical understanding.

The guide draws on a selection of the literature relating to teaching local history in schools, including that associated with successive versions of the National Curriculum. Examples of the learning and teaching approaches adopted are considered, along with matters arising. For the most part, the selection has been made to extend discussion of the themes covered in the exercises; no attempt has been made to provide a comprehensive review. However, as opportunity arises, mention is made of work that has been reported in relation to other themes. Attention is also drawn to the guidance provided both in the general literature relating to history teaching and in the scholarly publications dealing with the exercise themes. The intention is to demonstrate the value that each of these types of source can have in helping to plan and teach local history in effective and stimulating ways and from an informed standpoint.

The guide is divided into two parts. The first comprises four chapters dealing with general matters that arise in approaching local history teaching. Chapter 1 sets the scene by considering the nature of local history teaching and the forms it can take. The discussion emphasises the rich opportunities that studying local history can offer in developing children's historical knowledge and understanding, as well as their key skills, not least with regard to numeracy and literacy. The guiding principles that should govern learning and teaching in local history are also addressed. Chapter 2 discusses the types of written source material that can be used in teaching local history, commenting on their value and limitations. A similar approach is adopted in chapter 3, which deals with non-written sources. Chapter 4 is concerned with planning local history teaching. It is based around the notion of determining the types of historical understanding that children might attain, thereby giving purpose and direction to the investigations they undertake. Consideration is also given to the selection and adaptation that primary source material may require for classroom use.

The second part of the guide presents examples of classroom exercises in local history. The emphasis is on helping children to appreciate the nature of changes that have occurred over time at local level, as well as to deliberate on why change came about and the impact it had. The first two exercises are based on written sources. That in chapter 5 enables children to gain insights into how their forebears were educated during the late 19th and early 20th centuries, using evidence taken principally from school log books. The chapter 6 exercise shows how baptism register evidence can be used to determine forename popularity in the late Tudor era. It provides opportunity for children to compare local and national preferences regarding the names parents chose and to make comparisons with present-day name choices.

The remaining exercises focus on the use of non-written primary evidence in teaching local history. Chapter 7 presents an exercise that shows how children can work with visual evidence, in this case taken from a local stagecoach advertisement, to address the theme of road travel in early Victorian times. Chapter 8 considers a means by which children can gather oral testimony, with a view to helping them investigate aspects of local family life during the 1950s. In chapter 9, consideration is given to how children can use physical evidence to explore the ways in which housing standards changed for local families during the 19th century. The final chapter also deals with physical evidence, focusing on the artefacts that past generations in the locality have left. Each of these four chapters includes comment on other ways in which the type of evidence under consideration can be used in teaching local history, drawing on reported examples.

In devising the exercises, particular attention has been paid to the teaching approaches that can be used and the learning opportunities that arise. Consideration is also given to the ways in which the exercises might be developed. The exercises are intended to form components of study units that have either a local or a national focus. They might be incorporated directly into these units, wholly or in part, or replicated for other localities using the same types of source material and teaching approaches. Recreating the exercises adds to the immediacy of the investigations children undertake and enables them to compare their findings with those from another locality. With either approach, however, some adaptation of the exercises may well be needed to take account of the ages and abilities of the learners. The same points can be made about the related exercises appearing in the literature to which attention is drawn.

The guide is primarily intended for those who are new to local history teaching, whether established or recently-qualified classroom practitioners or participants in teacher-training courses. It should also be of use to undergraduate students who are undertaking work placements in schools, perhaps as part of modules that relate specifically to school history teaching. Hopefully, too, it will appeal to those working in the range of organisations that are involved with local history work in schools, including librarians, museum and art gallery curators and archivists, as well as parents and others who have an interest in how history is taught in schools.

Part I
Approaching learning and teaching in local history

Chapter 1
Local history: learning opportunities and principles

This chapter begins by considering how local history can be defined and the differing approaches that local historians adopt. Both are important matters in planning classroom activities that aim to develop children's historical skills and knowledge. Discussion then turns to how studying local history can help to meet the requirements of the National Curriculum and the GCSE awarding bodies. As will be seen, opportunities to incorporate a local dimension into historical studies abound and taking advantage of them can have a marked impact in social as well as academic terms. Finally, consideration is given to the principles that can be seen to underpin learning and teaching in local history in order to motivate children and to develop their historical understanding in meaningful ways.

What is local history?

The early National Curriculum documentation provides useful guidance in defining what is meant by local history, giving the following examples of localities:

- a village or rural area;
- a town or city or an area within a town or city;
- a county;
- or a region.[1]

The essential point here is that the study of local history need not, perhaps should not, take place within very constrained geographical limits, such as the immediate vicinity of the school. This is so because:

- useful opportunities for local study are likely to be missed by taking too narrow a geographical focus;
- the range and quality of local source material available for classroom use may be far more limited than it need be;
- local findings need to be placed in context in order to appreciate their historical significance.

Yet school environments may offer tremendous possibilities for studying aspects of local history. For instance, they may enable children to observe the features of houses built in, say, the inter-war or Victorian period. And even if these houses are newly built, their characteristics might still be studied and compared with older examples in the locality, leading to reflection on why change has occurred and the impact it has had.

---

1 National Curriculum Council, *History Non-Statutory Guidance* (NNC, 1991), p.C25.

A case can be made for approaching a local history theme at a county or regional level. A project dealing with the history of local immigration, for example, might want to address cultural diversity, a matter that, given varied intra-regional patterns of immigration, might be less tellingly approached if a limited geographical area is taken. But much will depend on the age of the children and on the theme being studied.

Types of local history

Two types of local history are commonly distinguished. They are:

- Local history that illustrates aspects of national or international history. The emphasis here is on the ways in which national or international developments impacted at local level, sometimes, but not always, in similar fashion. The effects of the 1832 Representation of the People Act on local male voting rights and disruptions that world wars brought to local families are cases in point.
- Local history in its own right. Concern here is with developments that have occurred within particular localities and that, to a greater or lesser extent, are distinctive. Examples include the varying development patterns of agricultural and industrial villages and of seaside resorts and industrial towns.[2]

With both types of local history contextualisation can, and should, occur in order to give significance to the findings made. As the examples above demonstrate, linking a local history study unit with more general events covered in the school history syllabus is one way forward in this respect. Starting at local level and then moving to national or international dimensions may be the preferred approach here.[3] Context can also be established by making comparisons between different localities at a point in time or within a particular locality over time. Family life in a town and nearby village during the 1950s is an example of the former and changes in family life in a village since the 1950s is an example of the latter.

Local history in schools has also been defined according to whether short-term or long-term coverage takes place. However, precisely what is meant by short- and long-term in this context is debatable. Studying, say, the changes that occurred to everyday life at local level during the Second World War would certainly comprise a short-period study, though effects lasting beyond the war years, such as rationing, might also be taken into account. Yet long-period local studies need not range across the centuries, with attempts to make them do so posing formidable challenges, not least with regard to generating learning resources. One way forward is to take a period that is long enough for appreciable changes to have occurred. Children can be led to articulate these changes, offer explanation for them and assess the impact they had. Maybe a period of a hundred years would be more than enough.

---

2 For a fuller discussion of this distinction, see W. B. Stephens, *Teaching Local History* (Manchester University Press, 1977), ch.1.

3 For discussion of this approach, see L. Dixon and A. Hales, *Bringing History Alive Through Local People and Places* (Routledge, 2014), especially chapters 6 and 8. See also P. Harnett and S. Whitehouse, 'Creative exploration of local, national and global links' in H. Cooper (ed), *Teaching History Creatively* (Routledge, 2013), ch.10.

Why teach local history in schools?

Much has been written on the value of teaching history at primary and secondary levels, in which the teaching of local history shares. One consideration is that children enjoy learning about the past, albeit to varying degrees and with differing emphases. Many wish to develop their historical interests and expertise as they grow older, with history being a popular subject at GCSE level and beyond. And local history has strong support amongst adults as a leisure time activity. Yet history teachers have to contend with the view that so-called 'vocational' subjects are of more value to children than subjects like history. Moreover, the charge can be made that local history is parochial in nature and is largely concerned with fact-finding rather than with historical interpretation. Accordingly, other arguments for studying history, including local history, have to be adduced. In considering them, however, sight should not be lost of the point that children may well attain greater success in taking subjects they enjoy than in those they do not.

One approach is to challenge the notion that studying history has little vocational significance. Plainly, this is not the case for those who enter professions where historical knowledge and understanding are crucial, including teaching, museum and archive work and the heritage industry. But the argument can be taken much further. By studying history, particularly through investigations making use of primary evidence - a key feature of local history work in schools - children can develop the type of intellectual skills that are of fundamental importance in a wide range of occupations. These skills include:

- locating and extracting information relating to a particular enquiry;
- evaluating the reliability of first-hand (primary) information;
- creating reasoned arguments based on evaluated evidence;
- communicating findings effectively, both in writing and orally;
- making critical evaluations of differing perspectives.

In developing these skills, a rich and varied range of source material relating to particular localities is available, providing ample scope for children to undertake their own investigations. Indeed, access to both oral testimony and evidence derived from examining the built environment is often more readily available for local than for more general historical studies. Additionally, developing social skills, including working constructively as part of a group, can be taken into account. All these skills, of course, can also prove invaluable outside the workplace as, for example, in deciding about which goods and services to purchase and for whom to vote for at political elections.

Mention of skills in communicating serves as a reminder that historical study of all types can play a crucial role in enhancing children's literacy skills, enabling them to present their findings in a variety of forms. In so doing, they gain experience in applying the grammatical conventions they have learned, in extending their vocabulary and in grappling with correct spelling. Writing up accounts of conversations undertaken with local people about aspects of their lives in the past provides an example. Furthermore, historical study offers a great deal of scope for children to engage with numeracy, the other subject that is generally given elevated status in the school curriculum. Both in analysing historical evidence and presenting historical findings, children can make use of the basic numeracy skills they have covered. As a result, their understanding of these skills is reinforced, as is their appreciation of the value of applying them in a variety of contexts. Interpreting numerical data, such as figures on population change relating to their own town or village, perhaps involving them in calculating decennial percentage changes, are cases in point. And in developing both their literacy and numeracy skills, children can make good use of ICT applications, spreadsheets amongst them.[4]

The study of past events and circumstances in their own right also has use value. Discovering how previous generations in a locality from all walks of life dealt with the situations in which they found themselves, and the actions they took, can prove both thought-provoking and instructive for children. These actions might involve, say, moral or pragmatic judgements, on which children can reflect and comment. Furthermore, studying the lives of past generations in a locality enables children to appreciate how their forebears' civil rights, including political engagement and religious tolerance, were acquired, often at immense personal sacrifice. They also learn about the responsibilities that go with these rights, legal and otherwise, including, for instance, that of voting in local and central government elections. Thus the historical study of a locality can play a primary role in fostering children's understanding about the nature and practice of citizenship. Additionally, studying the history of the organisations and institutions with which they are associated, including families and religious groups, as well as the localities in which they live, can play a major role in helping children to appreciate what characterises their own identities, and those of others, as well as the importance these identities have in shaping people's lives and actions.

Because of its association with the development of key skills, studying local history need not be confined to mere fact-finding. Nor need a parochial outlook prevail. As noted above, a key dimension of local history teaching and learning is that of establishing a context in which the results achieved can be viewed. Context may mostly be provided by adding a local dimension to more general historical study, but, as also noted above, comparative analysis within or between localities can achieve the same end.

National Curriculum requirements in local history

This section outlines the opportunities stated in the latest manifestation of the National Curriculum, which was introduced in 2014, and addresses matters that arise.[5] The requirements are set out in the table below.

Of the two types of local history outlined in the previous section, emphasis in the 2014 National Curriculum is on linkage with national developments that form part of the designated areas of study. However, at key stage 1, the example cited is related to the children's own locality, as is one of the examples given for each of key stages 2 and 3. How far this approach is feasible at these key stages will vary appreciably from one locality to another. Clearly, much will depend on how significant the locality was in pre-Norman times and whether sufficient source material is available on which teacher and taught can draw. But at least local history studies at each key

4 The links that history teaching can make with mathematics, languages and other subject areas are listed in H. Cooper, *The Teaching of History in Primary Schools* (David Fulton Publishers, third edition, 2000), pp.35-8.

5 The requirements can be seen by following the link to subject programmes of study at <https://www.gov.uk/government/collections/national-curriculum>.

stage can be based in the modern period, for which plentiful source material is available.

Key stage 1

Significant historical events, people and places in their own locality.

Key stage 2

A local history study

Examples (non-statutory)

- A depth study linked to one of the British areas of study listed above. (All of these are pre-1066.)
- A study over time tracing how several aspects of national history are reflected in the locality. (This can go beyond 1066.)
- A study of an aspect of history or a site dating from a period beyond 1066 that is significant in the locality.

Key stage 3

A local history study

Examples (non-statutory)

- A depth study linked to one of the British areas of study listed above. (They are all post-1066.)
- A study over time, testing how far sites in their locality reflect aspects of national history. (Some sites may predate 1066.)
- A study of an aspect or site in local history dating from a period before 1066.

The introductory statements that accompany each key stage of the revised history National Curriculum deal with such matters as promoting chronological understanding; engaging with the concepts of similarity and difference, change and continuity, causation and significance; creating understanding of how knowledge of the past is constructed from a range of sources; and being aware of different ways in which the past is represented. The statements are intended to demonstrate how children's historical understanding can be enhanced as they move through the key stages; in other words, how progression in this respect can be achieved. Thus, whereas at key stage 1, they are required only to understand how knowledge of the past is constructed from a range of sources, at key stage 3 they are expected to know how historical sources are 'used rigorously to make historical claims' and why differing interpretations of the past arise.

Local history teaching can readily engage with these matters. Moreover, it can do so with freedom of choice about the themes to address; with no need to be included as part of a chronological teaching approach; and, as chapters 2 and 3 demonstrate, with abundant primary source material to hand for classroom use. Accordingly, there is ample opportunity for children to be directly involved in historical investigation, helping them to develop the type of intellectual skills mentioned in the previous section. How progression might be achieved through local history teaching is considered in chapter 4.

Local history possibilities in GCSE syllabi

Since its inception in 1972, the *Schools History Project* has helped to promote the study of local history through its *History Around Us* component. A key aim in so doing has been to create awareness amongst pupils that 'the visible remains of the past around us are as important a resource for our understanding of history as written documents'. In introducing the component, the project team remarked on 'the lack of awareness about the visible evidence of the past which we "see" around us every day'. They continued:

> In this book we hope to provide some guidelines for teachers who want to prepare a course designed to help pupils study history by looking at their surroundings and identifying the remains of the past ... It involves the kind of work which is appropriate for pupils of a wide range of ages and abilities.

In linking locally-based study with the use of physical evidence, team members identified and considered a number of possible topics that could be undertaken, pointing to the various opportunities available. These topics were Prehistoric Britain; Roman Britain; castles and fortified manor houses; country houses; church buildings and furnishings; town development and domestic architecture; industrial archaeology; studies in the making of the rural landscape; and aspects of the history of the locality.[6]

The revisions to GCSE history courses applying from 2016 facilitate the approach pioneered in the *History Around Us* unit by permitting the study of 'one particular site in its historical context'. The site can range in scale from 'a particular building or part of a building to a city or rural landscape setting'. Students do not need to visit the site and, reflecting the differing approaches that can be adopted in local history teaching, the study can be linked with other parts of their GCSE course or stand alone.[7]

The specifications prepared by the Oxford, Cambridge and RSA Examinations awarding body (OCR) provide an example of the how the revision requirements have been translated into practice. Within stated parameters, schools have a completely free choice in selecting the site to be studied, which may be within walking distance or further afield; chosen from any time period; and iconic or relatively unknown. Additionally, fieldwork investigation at the site is seen to be desirable, though not a requirement. There is opportunity for both local study and fieldwork to be undertaken, therefore.[8]

Other GCSE courses that include local history elements are offered by OCR and by the Award Scheme Development and Accreditation Network (ASDAN). They are available at levels 1 and 2 of the National Qualifications Framework, so they can

6 Schools Council History 13-16 Project, *History Around Us: Some Guidelines for Teachers* (Holmes McDougall, 1976). The project's website is at <http://www.schoolshistoryproject.org.uk/index.php>.

7 Department for Education, *History GCSE Subject Content* (April, 2014). The document can be seen at <https://www.gov.uk/government/publications/gcse-history>.

8 The websites of the awarding bodies should be consulted for up-to-date details of the local history provision they make.

accommodate lower attainers. The OCR course is entitled *Applied History*. Students take four units from a choice of ten, four of which incorporate local history. They are:

> Local history - candidates prepare one or more assignments that involve an aspect of local history, demonstrating its significance and present-day relevance, as well as issues arising in carrying out the investigation.
>
> Heritage marketing – candidates plan the marketing of some aspect of British history, local or national, and produce examples of marketing materials using technology and multimedia presentations.
>
> Change over time – candidates investigate issues concerning the process, nature and extent of change over approximately 100 years. A local, national or international context may be taken.
>
> An archaeological enquiry – candidates carry out an enquiry into an historical issue that makes use of archaeological techniques. The enquiry can relate to any time period and may be local, national or global in scope.

The units need to be selected to produce a coherent course and one of the possibilities suggested relates to local history.

The ASDAN history provision falls within its range of short courses that focus on skills development. Local history comprises one of six course components. An example of the type of tasks set is shown below.

> What is 'the census'? Look at census returns for your area – it might be the street you live in, or where your school is. Create a spider diagram to illustrate what it tells you about the people who lived in that area at the time.

Guiding principles

Views may well differ among practitioners about the principles that should underpin local history teaching in schools. And even where commonality arises, varying degrees of emphasis may be given to the principles that are identified, in part, perhaps, to take account of the age and ability of those being taught. What follows, therefore, is a personal view, though it is much in accord with the perspectives rehearsed in the sources cited in the footnotes to this chapter.[9]

9 Stephens, *Teaching*, ch. 2; P. Knight, *History at Key Stages 1 & 2* (Longman, 1991), pp.63-6; T. Lomas, 'How do we ensure really good local history in primary schools?', *Primary History*, 30 (January, 2002), pp.4-6; 'Some learning and teaching strategies', *Primary History*, 25 (Summer, 2000), pp.14-17; and R. McFahn, S. Herrity and N. Bates, 'Riots, railways and Hampshire hill fort: exploiting local history for rigorous evidential enquiry', *Teaching History*, 134 (March, 2009), p.16. Also applying to teaching and learning in local history are the principles expounded by the *Nuffield Primary History Project.* They are: challenging children with an historical problem; teacher and pupils pose questions in meeting the challenge; study in depth; using authentic sources; being economical in the sources used; making sources accessible to children; and getting children to communicate their findings. For an application of these principles in relation to a classroom exercise in archaeology, see J. Dean, 'Nuffield Primary History and classroom archaeology', *Primary History*, 51 (Spring, 2009), pp.14-15. The project's website is at <http://www.nuffieldfoundation.org/nuffield-primary-history-0>.

To begin with, there is a need for children to engage with primary evidence. In part, this is because there is a general lack of secondary material on local history that is written with children in mind and that can be drawn upon to supplement the knowledge that teachers can provide from their own reading and investigation. But it is also because, as with studying other types of history, the primary evidence children use in their own investigations will help them to extend and deepen their historical knowledge and to appreciate and develop the skills, such as interpreting and evaluating evidence, required in undertaking effective historical study. However, in encouraging children to use primary sources, other considerations arise if meaningful learning outcomes are to be achieved.

Giving direction and challenge with regard to the investigations that children undertake are amongst them. Children might discover all sorts of fascinating pieces of information about their locality through using primary evidence and the interest generated in so doing cannot be entirely discounted as a teaching aid. But, particularly beyond key stage 1, setting a challenge that addresses a significant historical question or issue, perhaps to shed light on a national theme, becomes a requirement if children's historical understanding is to grow. For example, as part of an investigation into the nature of late Victorian schooling, a group of children might be asked to undertake an exercise using photocopied sheets from school log books to determine why scholars were absent from school. The task requires them to select evidence from that relating to other dimensions of school life and to communicate the findings they make. The challenge might also be formulated as a contentious hypothesis that the children can address, such as 'little attention was paid to girls' education during the Victorian period'.

Depth of study also enters into the account. Much can be achieved in this respect by encouraging children to examine carefully the evidence they use. Thus close observation of visual and physical sources will not only provide insights that are helpful to the investigation in hand, but will also enable questions to be asked that require children to infer. The questions accompanying the stagecoach illustration shown at the outset of chapter 7 provide examples. Further depth can be added to children's investigations if they are tasked to evaluate the reliability of the evidence they are using. For instance, as a starting point for discussion, they might be reminded that absenteeism details recorded in school log books represent head teachers' views and that the stagecoach illustration is an advertisement. Reality and interpretation might not entirely coincide.

Depth of analysis can also bring economy in generating resources for children to use. Effort is required, of course, to locate and prepare resources for teaching local history and to acquire a sufficient understanding of the topic in hand for teaching purposes. Yet quite limited amounts of well-chosen material will be sufficient for children to gain telling insights into the questions they address. The point is illustrated in chapter 6 with regard to the number of baptism entries required to carry out a children's forename exercise.

For planning purposes, there is much to be said for initially taking a broad-brush approach in identifying the themes within a topic that might be studied, but then narrowing down to just one or two of them for detailed investigation to take place. An example relating to school life in the past is given in chapter 4. The remaining themes can still enter into the teaching that takes place about the topic, but in other ways.

There is also the question of providing context for local history studies. Where the starting point is to assess the local impact of a national or international event, such as World War I, a context is clearly provided. However, if the starting point is the locality, considering, say, child labour in Victorian times, the historical significance of the findings can only be appreciated if some sort of comparison is made. More general findings relating to the country as a whole, or findings from other localities, are both possibilities. In other words, children can deal with contextual matters by engaging with the concept of similarity and difference. Equally, they might contextualise by comparing past with present, hence deliberating on continuity and change. With each of these approaches, they can also deepen analysis by seeking to explain the findings that result from the comparisons they make. Again, the children's name exercise in chapter 6 illustrates these approaches.

A final point to make is the emphasis that is placed on history, including local history, being essentially about people.[10] Numerous possibilities arise for children to examine the lives that past generations in their localities led and the contributions they made, within and beyond their families, irrespective of age, gender and the socio-economic group to which they belonged. Importantly, too, they can explore the varying attitudes and values that were espoused, not least in relation to politics and religion. Yet appreciating the nature of the built environment in which they led their lives is also a requirement if the problems they faced and the aspirations they held are to be understood. Connecting people with place brings obvious links with the Geography curriculum, concerning such matters as the way people use their localities and how people in localities connect with people elsewhere.[11]

Conclusion

Studies that are locally based can add a valuable dimension to history teaching in schools, as long as they deal with themes that have historical significance and the findings that emerge are adequately contextualised. They enable children of all ages and abilities to undertake investigations that can involve non-documentary as well as documentary sources; that can draw on a wide range of themes; and that can permit in-depth studies that enhance historical understanding, develop key skills and generate original insights. Support for them as a component of history programmes of study at key stages 1-3 continues to be offered by the National Curriculum, as has been the case since its inception. Provision is also made by the awarding bodies for local history to feature in GCSE courses. So, the opportunity to teach local history in schools is considerable and, as will become increasingly apparent in the chapters that follow, plenty of advice is available on the varied and stimulating approaches that can be adopted in so doing.

10 For a succinct discussion of this point, see A. Blyth, et.al., *Place, Time and Society 8-13: Curriculum Planning in History, Geography and Social Science* (Collins, 1976), pp.55-7.

11 For further detail on this theme, including suggestions of coverage at key stages 1 and 2, see S. Catling, 'Geography and history: exploring the local connection', *Primary History*, 42 (Spring, 2006), pp.14-6.

Chapter 2
Written sources for local history

Assuming the geographical area and time period are not too narrowly defined, schools can draw on a wide range of source material to facilitate local history teaching. In discussing these sources, a distinction is made between those that, for the most part, are in written form and those that are non-written. No attempt is made to provide comprehensive coverage, a task that would be Herculean in scale.[12] Instead, discussion centres on the types of material that are generally available at local level and that have high use value in the classroom. In dealing with written sources, this chapter covers historians' publications (secondary sources) and information left by contemporaries (primary sources). Examples of them are given and comment is made on their significance for teaching purposes. The crucial role played by local libraries in providing written source material is emphasised, though attention is also drawn to other means of accessing it, particularly online.

Secondary sources

Whilst a tremendous amount of local history has been published in book, booklet and article forms, as well as online, its academic quality, and hence its worth in teaching, varies appreciably. Much of it is written at a popular level and does not rest on a sound consideration of the available evidence. Nor may it say much about the sources used. Yet by no means is all of it open to such criticism. Some is the product of detailed investigation by very competent local historians and though it may lack contextualisation, it may still provide extremely useful insights. And this can be the case both with publications that may seem to be dated, as well as with recent ones.[13] Additionally, academic local history studies that are well contextualised, including unpublished higher-degree theses, have come to form a sizable body of literature and may be of considerable help in devising investigations that children can undertake.

Growing amounts of secondary material relating to the history of localities is becoming available online. The following are important examples.

12 Scholarly works that consider a wide range of local history sources and their uses include W. B. Stephens, *Sources for English Local History* (Manchester University Press, 1973); P. Riden, *Local History: A Handbook for Beginners* (Batsford, 1983); K. Tiller, *English Local History: An introduction* (Sutton, 2002); and P. Carter and K. Thompson, *Sources for Local Historians* (Phillimore, 2005).

13 Amongst books that might appear to be dated is Islay Doncaster's *Finding the History Around Us* (Blackwell, 1957). However, the book was written with teachers in mind and contains brief histories of Birmingham and Brighton, showing the types of sources she used. Her approach might be followed with profit for other towns. She also lists long-term changes in church architecture (with illustrations) and in the interior design and contents of castles and country houses, along with the dress of those in residence.

Victoria County History (VCH)

The VCH volumes provide detailed, scholarly histories of English counties covering general themes, including religion, politics, demography and industry, as well as places within counties. The VCH was founded in 1899 and its work is ongoing. In some instances, histories of individual places can be viewed online. So, too, can examples of teaching resources and lesson plans, which are contained in the *Schools Learning Zone* section of the VCH's website. These relate to particular localities, but the point is made that they can act as models for teaching across the country. Examples of themes covered are the *History of Agriculture in Wiltshire,* which starts in the Iron Age and comes through to recent times, and *Religious Sites of Cornwall,* which is concerned with the establishment of Christianity in Cornwall, Cornish saints and how the present system of places of worship in the county evolved. These resources can be viewed at <http://www.victoriacountyhistory.ac.uk/about>.

The VCH volumes contain local population figures derived from decennial census schedules. Those for part of Buckinghamshire are shown below.

Parish	Acreage	1801	1811	1821	1831	1841	1851	1861	1871	1881	1891	1901
Ashendon Hundred												
Ashendon . . .	2,128	248	319	339	368	312	290	325	274	237	199	212
Aston Sandford ‡ .	679	71	76	84	82	86	88	59	58	59	48	46
Boarstall	3,078	179	188	231	268	252	243	255	244	209	188	151
Brill †	3,109	859	864	1,060	1,283	1,449	1,311	1,432	1,353	1,289	1,251	1,206
Chearsley ‡ . . .	943	214	217	263	337	308	292	287	311	235	242	212
Chilton ‡	2,069	316	338	379	314	364	398	364	336	301	287	285
Claydon, East . .	2,396	299	309	339	336	378	361	385	376	341	343	336
Claydon, Middle .	2,640	103	129	160	136	127	165	146	139	225	227	231
Crendon, Long[2] † ‡	3,461	991	989	1,212	1,382	1,656	1,700	1,570	1,365	1,179	1,187	1,075
Dorton	1,477	105	124	133	158	151	139	137	125	111	137	140
Fleet Marston[3] ‡ .	934	—	46	43	41	38	30	23	37	27	51	53
Grandborough ‡ .	1,580	230	251	286	341	345	359	374	367	300	301	297
Grendon Underwood † ‡	2,536	285	271	312	379	384	427	451	448	365	373	323
Hogshaw with Fulbrook	1,322	55	55	68	48	50	50	50	61	62	78	56
Ickford (part of)[4] .	1,025	271	308	324	382	374	398	416	398	354	345	319
Ilmer †	684	74	69	68	78	79	82	79	70	63	48	51
Kingsey (part of)[5] †	915	165	169	204	222	178	202	171	145	151	124	85

Source: W. Page (ed.), *Victoria History of the County of Buckingham, vol. II* (1908) p.96.

British Association for Local History (BALH)

The Education section of the BALH website includes resources dealing with the theme of local history and the First World War. The resources mainly comprise an on-going series of short articles that have appeared in the Association's *Local History News.* The articles, which can be viewed online without charge, examine key topics and questions that arise in studying the First World War, along with the sources and methods used to investigate them. Each is written by an expert in the field. Topics addressed include Catriona Pennell's *Community Responses to the Outbreak of War,* which challenges the notion that 'populations in the belligerent countries were jingoistically enthusiastic for war' and Tim Lomas' *Schools in the First World War,* which poses a range of questions about the impact the war had on schooling and provides examples of evidence from various parts of the country that can be used to address them. Other topics covered in the series include women and work; food; memorials of war; the agricultural community at war; children; soldiers' letters from the front; and London.

The Local Historian, a journal published three times a year by the Association, contains articles that deal especially with applying the principles and methods used in studying local history. Some of the articles engage with themes that may form local history study units in schools, or parts of them, and can provided invaluable help in their preparation. Some are based on particular localities, but, in common with the VCH teaching resources, they can reveal insights that raise matters of more general concern, as well as providing comparative material for children to use in studying their own localities.[14] Examples include:

K. Lawrence, 'How accurate are the nineteenth century British censuses? Using parliamentary reports as an external standard', vol. 45, 3 (2015)

J. Becket, 'Rethinking the English village', vol. 42, 4 (2012)

H. Jones, 'British Cities: 'Celebrating and commemorating the Second World War', vol. 42, 1 (2012)

M. Huggins, 'The local history of sport: approaches, sources and methods', vol. 42, 2 (2012)

D. Killingray, 'Immigrant communities and British local history', vol. 41, 1 (2011)

B. White, '"Sowing the seeds of patriotism": The Women's Land Army in Devon, 1916-18', vol. 41, 1 (2011)

M. Curtis, 'Education in a nineteenth century Oxfordshire village', vol. 41, 3 (2011)

M. Bullock, 'The Women's Land Army in the Craven District of Yorkshire during the Second World War', vol. 40, 2 (2010)

D. Hunter, 'Making ends meet: household strategies in the East Riding in the mid-nineteenth century', vol. 40, 1 (2010)

The BALH website is at <http://www.balh.org.uk/>.

BBC local history trails

This website contains trails that provide introductions to the sources and methods used in historical investigation. One deals specifically with local history, covering the themes of industry, landscape, the village and the city. A case study approach is adopted, noting the types of questions that can be asked and ways in which investigations can be undertaken.

Local history elements can also be found in some of the other trails; those on

14 Individual copies can be purchased from BALH and local libraries may be subscribers to the journal.

Victorian Britain and *How To Do History* are amongst them. Links are given to sources and to organisations that can provide further help. The website is at <http://www.bbc.co.uk/history/trail/local_history/>.

BBC Legacies

This site centres on the themes of architectural heritage, immigration and emigration, myths and legends and work and occupations. The themes comprise case studies relating to localities in various parts of the UK. In some instances, the case studies contain personal stories relating to them. The temporal coverage is wide. For example, the Wiltshire case study on immigration and emigration deals with the Beaker Folk, who are thought to have first come to Britain about 4,500 years ago. Examples of case studies relating to the work theme include the textile industry of the Scottish Borders; commercial life in Roman Colchester; and the mechanisation of the Northampton shoe-making industry. Links are again given to further online resources. Thus the slate quarrying case study on North Wales has a link to the *Slateside* website, which provides details on a various aspects of the Welsh slate industry. The site materials can be viewed at <http://www.bbc.co.uk/legacies/>.

The secondary literature on local history will be of most value in providing the background knowledge and understanding required for teaching purposes; it is unlikely to have been written with children in mind. Yet extracts from it, as well as awareness of the sources and approaches used in its preparation, are likely to be considerable use in developing classroom activities.[15]

Printed primary sources

Whilst the primary sources outlined in this and the following chapter have a tremendous amount to offer in facilitating local history teaching, it must be appreciated that the evidence they yield might not be entirely reliable and questions should be asked about possible bias, inaccuracy and incompleteness. Indeed, these are matters that children should be able to address with growing confidence and expertise as they move through the key stages, learning to be wary about taking at face value the evidence that the sources provide. Asking questions about who produced the sources and why will help them greatly in this respect.

Local newspapers

These occur for some districts prior to the 19th century, though they may not contain much local material. As the 19th century progresses, the number of local newspapers increases, especially after the repeal of stamp duty in 1860. So, too, does the local detail they contain. Local newspapers cover a wide variety of matters, including the state of trade; accidents; crimes committed and punishments carried out; weather conditions; social events; court proceedings; sport; and elections. The advertisements they contain can be useful, too. Details of property sales and annual letting of the tolls collected on turnpike roads are examples. Local libraries

15 Martin Spafford used material taken mainly from a reputable local history book on Leyton in East London to prepare his own booklet for use with a Year 9 class. The booklet contained a range of extracts drawing on various types of evidence. For further details of the booklet and the project to which it related, see M. Spafford, 'Thinking about local history', *Teaching History*, 149 (December, 2012), pp.4-7.

may have indexes available, as well as books of newspaper cuttings. They also keep micro-film copies of newspapers for their areas and may provide access to online collections of local newspapers, including the *British Newspaper Archive.*[16]

MISCELLANEOUS SALES

A.R.P. SUPPLIES.
BARKER'S POOL (opposite City Hall);
54, LONDON ROAD, and
77, FITZWILLIAM ROAD, ROTHERHAM.

OFFICIAL RESPIRATOR BAGS, SAND BAGS,
HAVERSACKS and CONTAINERS.

TRADE SUPPLIED.

A.R.P.—IRON DOORS for Air Raid Shelters, splinter proof and rubber jointed, standard sizes in stock; all kinds of A.R.P. wrot iron work made to instructions.—Alfred Shaw and Son, Ltd., 26, Duke st, Sheffield, 2.

A.R.P.—Steel Angle skeleton construction, trench reinforcement and shelter framework, 6ft. long, 5ft. wide; £1.—Garside, Throstle Nest, Farsley, Leeds, S.

A.R.P. Stock of SAND for Sand Bags available. —Apply: Middleton Mining Co., Ltd., Estate Office, Middleton-by-Youlgrave. Tele. Youlgrave 9.

A.R.P. WOODWORK.—Dressing Stations, Forms for Shelters.—Mackenzie's, Bernard rd.

FIRE EXTINGUISHERS.—We have still in stock a few Foam, Soda Acid, and Carbon Tetrochloride.—'Phone 41131.

FOLDING IRON CAMP BED, complete, 35s., a few left.—Roberts, Firvale. 36077.

On With the Show Demand

Theatres Ready to Open

THE box office of the Lyceum Theatre, Sheffield, is now open for dealing with the many inquiries as to the prospects of the reopening of the theatre.

If the Home Office agree to places of entertainment in vulnerable areas being opened again, it is not expected that Sheffield authorities will put any obstacle in the way of audiences being permitted to assemble within specified hours.

"It is quite obvious that the blackened streets and the lack of entertainment are likely in time to affect adversely the health of the public in general," said Mr. A. E. Holland, manager of the Lyceum Theatre, to a "Telegraph and Independent" reporter.

Source: *Telegraph and Independent*, Sheffield, Thursday, September 14th, 1939.

These extracts help children to appreciate the marked disruption to everyday life that, from its outset, World War II was bringing to local people and the steps they were taking in response. Both extracts relate to the threat of bombing. The advertisement gives details of how householders were trying to guard against its effects. The article shows how the theatre manager, understandably wishing to protect his livelihood, sought to make his case by arguing that theatre going would bring health benefits.

Local public health reports

These often date from the mid-19th century, many being compiled prior to local boards of health being formed. They give graphic, often disgusting, descriptions of insanitary housing conditions, as well as comments on inadequacies in water supply, sewerage systems, burial grounds and road conditions. Statistical data is also recorded, including birth and death rates and population and house totals.

16 *Richard Heaton's Newspaper Collection* contains transcribed extracts from selected local newspapers in various parts of England. It can be viewed at <http://freepages.genealogy.rootsweb.ancestry.com/~dutillieul/ZOtherPapers/Index.html>.

Coverage tends to be partial, with the worst parts of towns and villages being noted. But the reports deal with places that relied on the conservancy system of domestic sanitation rather than the water-carriage system (WC). In other words, ordure accumulations, often contained in open cesspits adjoining back-yard privies, had to be removed from houses by manual means. Details are given in chapter 9. Libraries are likely to have original copies of public health reports for their localities.

> Mrs. Rodger's property, behind Mill-gate, occupied by John Wolstenholme, has no privy; the tenant pays all rates, except water, for which 2*d.* per week is included in the rent of 6*l.* 10*s.* The house contains only two bed-rooms, for husband, wife, six children, and a young man, who lives with them. One of the children is blind from small-pox, and another has an eruption on the face. The wife says they are sometimes without water for two or three days.
>
> There are two houses in the market-place without any privies.

Source: William Lee, *Report to the General Board of Health on ... Rotherham and Kimberworth* (1851).

> *Barford-street.*—There is an open ditch here full of cesspool refuse, built up to on both sides. In No. 15 Court in this street, there is an open filthy drain on the surface; the house next to the privy has fever at the present time. The open ditch here cost 45*l.*, in two years, to clean it; it might have been permanently sewered for much less money. The Commissioners clean it, but have no power to sewer and cover it. The land is covered with rubbish, and all open and unpaved.

Source: Robert. Rawlinson, *Report to the General Board of Health on ... the Borough of Birmingham* (1849).

The Lee extract highlights overcrowding and that some houses did not have a privy. It might also be noted that some contemporaries disliked houses with only two bedrooms on moral grounds, implying that boys and girls should have separate bedrooms. The Rawlinson extract points to open ditches into which privies drained and raises the theme of the cost savings that it was claimed would arise from providing adequate sewers.

Trade directories

Some date from the 18th century or before, but are much more frequent thereafter. They may cover an entire county, an individual town, or a group of neighbouring towns; in some cases, town directories also cover the neighbouring rural districts. Designed primarily to give information to businessmen, trade directories vary in the amount and type of detail they contain, but become fuller with time. Alphabetical lists of businesses and of local notables occur, along with classified lists of businesses and street directories. The times and venues of transport and postal services are also featured, as well as advertisements, some with visuals, and population data obtained from decennial censuses. They may give local histories, too. The descriptions of towns they provide tend to eulogise, giving different perspectives from those offered in public health reports, a matter that children might well investigate.[17]

17 For further details of the availability of trade directories and discussion of their uses in

WILLIAM KNEE,

General Haulier, 148, Temple Street, Bristol.

LARGE AND COMMODIOUS

SPRING VANS,

FOR

REMOVING FURNITURE, &c., &c.,

WITHOUT PACKING, TO ANY PART OF THE KINGDOM.

W. KNEE calls the attention of the Public to his long and extensive Vans, which are not to be equalled in the world, for lightness and convenience for the Removal of Goods, with Safety, and without Packing,—being built at a great expense for the express purpose. This is worthy of notice to Parties Removing, as it will insure them the Safety of Property from those Accidents which are likely to occur by repeated Loading and Unloading by Rail or Water. His Vans are also conveniently fitted up for the Removal of Chimney Glasses.

SMALL VANS AND SPRING CARTS.

Spacious Dry Warerooms for Housing Furniture for any period.

Source: *Matthews's Almanack* (Bristol, 1851).

The vans shown were sizeable, requiring six horses to pull them. Risk of damage to goods during transit was lessened because the vans were covered; they were fitted with springs to give a smooth ride; and goods could be delivered from door to door without transhipment, as had to be the case with canals and railways. Knee claimed his vans were 'conveniently fitted up' for moving chimney glasses – tall glasses fitted to oil lamps.

Trade directories show the wide range of industries that emerged in towns and the numerical importance of businesses run by individuals and partnerships. The classified lists they give can be used selectively to indicate the growth of local industries over time. However, concerns arise as to the completeness of the lists.

---

studying local history, see G. Shaw and A. Tipper, *British Directories* (Mansell, second edition, 1997). Coverage is of England and Wales (1850-1950) and Scotland (1773-1950).

246 MATHEWS's DIRECTORY.—1845.

Coach Lamp Makers.

Hall & Peddar, 2 Barrs street
Hall H. R. 2 Lower Castle st
Tovey J. 4 Parade, St James's

Coach Currier & Patent Leather Dresser.

Burgess W. 9 Small street

Coach Builders.

Barton S. & J. & Sons, near Stone Bridge, St. Augustine's back, and Nelson street
Crouch T. 110 Temple street
Fuller —, 9 & 91 Limekiln lane, and 60 College street
Jordan W. H. Cumberland basin
Hill W. Temple street
Kemp J. & Son, Limekiln lane
Parrett H. Hotwell road
Perry & Perrott, 40 Thomas st.
Perry & Clark, Stoke's croft and Limekiln lane
Perry T. & J. 41 and 61 Stoke's croft
Phillips F. 34 Limekiln lane
Pritchard & Craymer, 15 Thomas street
Rogers W. College place
Webb B. Stapleton road
Williams J. Coronation road
Williams W. Temple gate, and Broad street, Bath
Williams Wm. Cheltenham road

Coach Brass Founder.

Barber R. 94 Thomas street

Coach Proprietors.

Bland John, 60 Broadmead—
Folwell Edward, Upper York st
Niblett I. White Lion, Broad st each of the above furnish black coaches for funerals to all parts
Holder Wm. Horsefair
Pring B. St. Michael's hill

Coal Merchants.

Baker H . Canons' marsh
Baker T. C. 85 Quay
Brain Wm. & Co. back West st
Carpenter Charles, Redcliff back
Chaplin R. Cumberland basin
Farley Thomas, Cheese lane
Foord Wm. Temple back
Glass W. Temple back
Gummer F. near Ashton gate
Hammond J. Temple back
Headford & Sage, Upper Easton
Hewitt W. Queen street
Hewitt C. H. & J. Lower Rail-road wharf, St. Philip's—Coal-Pit-Heath Co.—for exportation
Hood, Lambert, & Co. Temple [back
Johns W. Meadow st
Jones J. Rownham, Hotwells
Knight G. St. Philip's—wharf Avon street
Knight J. Bread st. St. Philip's
Leonard, Boult, & Co. Lower Easton colliery
Leonard, Jefferis, & Co. Bitton
Naish Wm. & Son, Grove
Newton & Traloar, Wapping wrf
Pitt W. A. Redcliff back
Poole J. jun. Hotwell road, and St. Stephen's wharf, Quay
Pope R. & Co. Temple back
Rennolds J. West st. Bedminster
Rennolds S. West st. Bedminster
Ring R. E. Temple back
Russell T. Lower Montague st
Russell Wm. Thomas st. Kingsdn
Stanton H. Temple back
Stanton W. & Co. Butts wharf, St. Augustine's, and Rownham wharf, Hotwells (late Jones)
Stratton W. H. Queen st Castle st
Stratton W. 24 Wilson st
Timsbury Coal Co.—Agent, C. Clark, 39 Bridge st
Tothill H. Temple back
Waters and Rennolds, back of West street

Coffee Houses.

Ashton J. 17 Narrow Wine st
Atkins J. E. 54 Broad street
Davey G. 7 Nicholas street
Giraud J. Bath street
Jones B. J. 52 Broad street
Mayne B. T. 38 Thomas street
Morgan C. Bath parade

Source: *Matthews's Almanack* (Bristol, 1845).

Searchable copies of a selection of trade directories from localities throughout England and Wales can be found at <http://www.historicaldirectories.org/hd/index.asp>. They cover various years from the 1760s to the 1910s. However, local libraries will have a more complete coverage for their own areas.

Parliamentary papers

Available from the late 18th century, these comprise a range of records arising from the activities of the Houses of Parliament. Of particular use in local history are Commons sessional papers, which include reports from parliamentary committees (e.g. Health of Towns, 1840); commissions (e.g. Children's Employment, 1842); and periodic reports (e.g. quarterly and half-yearly reports of the factory inspectors from 1835 onwards). Most of the papers give nationwide coverage, but they provide a great deal of information at local and regional levels, often reporting the testimony of informed local witnesses.

Source: Parliamentary Papers, *Children's Employment Commission (Mines), 1842: Bradford and Leeds*. The report can be viewed on the website of The Coalmining History Resource Centre at http://www.cmhrc.co.uk/site/home/index.html>. Edited reports for coalfields elsewhere in Britain are also included on the site.

The sketch shows Ann Ambler and William Dyson (aged 14) being wound from the pit bottom to the surface by means of a hand-operated winch. They sat cross-lapped on what was termed a clatch iron. In relation to this and other working practices, issues of morality as well as of safety brought concern. The children worked at Ditchfield & Clay's colliery, Elland. West Yorkshire.

Extracts from the 1842 report, including illustrations, are contained in a book entitled *The Condition and Treatment of the Children Employed in the Mines and Collieries of the United Kingdom*. Extracts from the book relating to several localities can be viewed on the British Library website at <http://www.bl.uk/collection-items/report-on-child-labour-1842>.

Medical officer of health reports

These reports are normally available from the later decades of the 19th century, the 1875 Public Health Act requiring urban and rural local authorities to appoint legally-qualified doctors as medical officers of health. But some local authorities took this step well before the Act was passed. This was the case in London, for example, where appointments in some boroughs date as far back as the mid-19th century. The reports made for London boroughs have been digitised under the heading *London's Pulse: Medical Officer of Health Reports, 1848-1972*. See the Wellcome Trust library website at <http://wellcomelibrary.org/moh/>. For other localities, libraries keep copies.

A wide range of information is available in the reports on public health matters, including details on epidemics, birth and death rates, sanitation and water supply. They are very helpful for assessing change over time when used with early Victorian public health reports.

Folio No.	*Street.*	*Ward No.*	*Age*	*Sex*	*Closet Accommodation.*	*Paving of Yard.*	*Paving of Passages.*	*Remarks.*
98	Nursery Road, Cheadle Heath	9	5½	M.	Do.	Partly flagged	—	House damp. Dilapidated privy midden.
99	Robinson Street	9	7	F.	Privy midden	Flagged	Flagged	Wet and offensive privy midden.
108	Bann Street	8	1½	F.	Do.	Partly flagged	Do.	Fatal.
109	Buxton Road	14	5¾	M.	Pail closet	Flagged......	—	Kitchen sink waste pipe untrapped, since repaired.
122	Infirmary (Union Street)	7 11	8 ms.	F..	W.C. outside	—	—	Fatal. Back-to-back house in filthy state; sink waste pipe appears to be connected direct with drain.
149	Greg Street, South Reddish	16	8	F.	Do.	Partly flagged	—	—
177	Bordon Road	9	3½	M.	Do.	Partly tiled...	Earth	Fatal.
180	Coronation Street, South Reddish	16	4½	F.	Do.	Flagged	—	Fatal.

EXISTING SANITARY ACCOMMODATION.

Districts.	No. of Privy Seats.	No. of Privy Ashpits.	No. of Separate Ashpits.	No. of Waste Water Closets.	No. of Pails.	Satisfactory Water Closets.
No. 1	·69	241	257	86	224	21,920
,, 2	611	343	374	83	18	
,, 3	978	587	605	456	12	
,, 4	624	313	334	143	22	
,, 5	176	108	371	22	17	
Total...	2858	1592	1941	790	293	

Source: County Borough of Stockport, *Annual Report of the Medical Officer of Health* (1910), p.34 and (1914), p.68.

The 1910 extract reports the insanitary conditions of several houses in which diphtheritic disease occurred. Young children were the victims, four of whom died. Examples of domestic sanitation are given. The 1914 extract notes domestic sanitary provision in various parts of the town at a time when water closets were gradually replacing privies with ashpits - some of them shared between families - and pail closets. Exercises on domestic sanitation are considered in chapter 9.

Travellers' observations

Those journeying in Britain during times past have left details both about their experiences as travellers and about the places they visited. As an example of the former, an extract from a letter written by Arthur Young, the agricultural reformer, during his tour of southern Britain in 1769, may be quoted. He travelled mainly along turnpike (toll) roads, some of which, including those in South Wales, he viewed with profound disfavour.[18]

> But my dear Sir, what am I to say of the roads in this country! The turnpikes! ... From Chepstow to the half-way house between Newport and Cardiff, they continue mere rocky lanes, full of hugeous stones as big as one's horse, and abominable holes. The first six miles from Newport, they were so detestable, and without either direction-posts, or mile-stones, that I could not well persuade myself I was on the turnpike, but had mistook the road; and therefore asked everyone I met, who answered me, to my astonishment, Ya-as.

Young and other travellers made favourable as well as critical comment about the road conditions they encountered, pointing to the marked variation that could occur.

As to the comments travellers made about the places they visited, an extract from Daniel Defoe's tour of Britain, which he undertook during the 1720s, may be taken.[19] Citing Deptford, he notes how several villages had become joined

18 A. Young, *A Six Weeks Tour through the Southern Counties of England and Wales* (1769), pp.153-4. The book can be seen online at <https://archive.org/details/asixweekstourthooyougoog>.

19 D. Defoe, *A Tour Through the Whole Island of Great Britain* (1986 reprint of 1724-6 edition),

to London's streets 'by continued building' as the city expanded outwards. He developed the theme in relation to Islington.

> The town of Islington, on the north side of the city, is in like manner joined to the streets of London, excepting one small field, and which in itself is so small, that there is no doubt, but in a very few years, they will be entirely joined, and the same may be said of Mile-End, on the east side of the town.

By using local maps from different time periods, children may be able to discover if a town or towns in their locality grew in the manner Defoe observed. They might also be able to see how urban gardens and other open spaces were built upon as towns grew, helping to create some very crowded living conditions.

Hand-written primary sources

Census enumerators' schedules

Available for each census year from 1841 (when they were first introduced) to 1911 (one hundred years elapse before there is public access to them) census enumerators' schedules comprise copies of the standardised, printed forms that householders were required to complete on census day. The forms were distributed to households by local enumerators. The enumerators collected the completed forms, giving help if required, and then copied the information given into their books.[20] Copies of the original schedules can be seen on microfilm at local libraries.

Parish or Township of Salesbury		Ecclesiastical District of St Peter's					City or Borough of	Town of	Village of Copster Green
No. of Householder's Schedule	Name of Street, Place, or Road, and Name or No. of House	Name and Surname of each Person who abode in the house, on the Night of the 30th March, 1851	Relation to Head of Family	Condition	Age of Males	Age of Females	Rank, Profession, or Occupation	Where Born	Whether Blind, or Deaf-and-Dumb
4		Henry Howarth	Head	Widr	62		Hand Loom Weaver Cotton	Lancashire Clayton	
		Alice Do	Daur	U		25	Hand Loom Weaver	Do Salesbury	
		Jane Do	Daur	U		23	Do	Do	
		Thomas Do	Son	U	18		Do	Do	
		Mary Do	Daur	U		15	Do	Do	
		Mary Hayhurst	Grandaur			8		Do	
5		John Whinkley	Head	Widr	66		Hand Loom Weaver Cotton	Blackburn	
		Betty Do	Daur	U		34	Hand Loom Weaver	Lancashire Salesbury	
		Joseph Do	Grandson	U	15		Do	Do	
6		Hannah Slater	Head	W		36	Do	Do	
		Do Do	Daur	U		13	Do	Do	
		Daniel Slater	Son	U	11		Do	Do	
7		Robert Barn	Head	Mar	59		Hand Loom Weaver	Do	
		Mary Do	Wife	Mar		60	Do	Do Billington	
		Robert Do	Son	Widr	32		Excavator	Do Salesbury	
		Henry Do	Son	U	19		Hand Loom Weaver	Do Salesbury	
		Robert Do	Grandson	U	7		Scholar	Do Claytonledale	

Source: 1851 census schedule, Salesbury, enumeration district 3b.

p.287.

20 For further details of the duties of census enumerators and how they operated, see G. Timmins, *Working Life and the First Modern Census*, a contribution to the BBC's *History Trails: Victorian Britain* web pages at <http://www.bbc.co.uk/history/trail/victorian_britain/>. Take the *Earning a Living* link. More general discussion on censuses taken during the 19th century can be found in E. Higgs, *Making Sense of the Census Revisited: Census Records for England and Wales, 1801-1901* (Institute of Historical Research, 2005).

Salesbury is a rural settlement situated in the Ribble valley to the north-east of Blackburn in Lancashire. As the census extract suggests, its economy still depended strongly on handloom weaving in the mid-19th century. Using census schedule information, children can prepare frequency distributions relating to birth place, occupations and age/sex.

The schedules give details of individuals, including names, occupations, age and gender, marital status, relationship to head of household (except 1841) and birth place. More detail was required over time, including, from 1901, whether people worked at home. The completed schedules form the basis of the printed census returns noted above.[21] It is important to be aware that census schedules present snap-shot pictures at specific dates, though comparison between different census years can be used to reveal changes and continuities. And point-in-time analysis with census data can be valuable, as in comparing the life styles of a sample of well-to-do and ordinary families in the Victorian era, especially if physical and large-scale map evidence relating to the sample can also be utilised.

School log books

The 1862 Revised Code required head teachers of schools receiving annual government grants to keep daily a log book (or diary). They were supposed to make in it

> the briefest entry which will suffice to specify either ordinary progress, or whatever other fact concerning the school or its teachers, such as the dates of withdrawals, commencements of duty, cautions, illnesses, etc., may be required to be referred to at a future time, or may otherwise deserve to be recorded.

No 'reflections or opinions of a general character' were to be included, nor any entry deleted.[22] During their annual school visits, inspectors were to examine the log books to ensure they were properly kept.

Considerable variation occurred in the way head teachers interpreted these instructions. Some confined themselves to brief comments of a factual nature, preferring to make weekly rather than daily comments; others wrote in considerable detail about events that occurred, some relating to their personal lives, and did not shirk from giving their opinions about them, albeit from their perspectives. What emerges is a wealth of evidence about school matters, including the curriculum; buildings and classroom equipment; inspections; policies on lateness; pupil teachers and monitors; attendance and behaviour of pupils; and special events.[23]

Facsimile copies of school log books for the abandoned Scottish islands of Mingulay and St. Kilda, the former dating from 1875 to 1910 and the latter from 1901 to 1930, can be found online at <http://www.nas.gov.uk/about/110908.

21 Further details can be found on the website of the Society of Genealogists at <http://www.sog.org.uk/learn/help-getting-started-with-genealogy/guide-four/>.

22 These instructions can sometimes be found pasted inside the front cover of log books.

23 Further examples of the insights that log books provide into school life are outlined in S. Wood, 'Social history from school log books', *The Local Historian*, 14 (1981), pp.471-6. The author draws on evidence from Aberdeenshire schools.

219

3rd October. The attendance, which at one time was so satisfactory in this department, has recently been uniformly poor. During last quarter we did not once reach 90 per cent for any week.
This week the percentage is only 87.2.
I was absent Tuesday and Wednesday this week owing to back-ache.

Source: Log book of Richardson Dees Senior School, Wallsend, near Newcastle-upon-Tyne. The source, which relates to a theme on schools at the turn of the 20th century, can be viewed on the Primary Sources website at <http://www.primarysources.org.uk/source-details.php?source_id=238>.

The extract is reproduced with permission of Tyne and Wear Archives, ref. E.WA912. It shows the concern head teachers had about attendance, which could be disrupted for varied reasons. The matter is considered in chapter 5.

asp>. Some the entries made are very detailed. Also available online are extracts from the log book of Farmer Road School in Leyton, East London. They relate mostly to the First and Second World War years. Comments on the value of log book entries in teaching are given, including the observation that in terms of language and content they are generally accessible to most ability levels. They can be viewed at <http://educationforum.ipbhost.com/ topic/2041-school-log-books-as-historical-sources/>. Eric Gadd, *Victorian Logs* (1979) contains a transcription of the log books from Northam Junior School, Southampton for the years 1863 to 1877. Additionally, Jacqui Halewood has drawn attention to some moving log book extracts showing child poverty amongst the pupils attending Bishop Graham Memorial Ragged School, Chester during the late Victorian era.[24]

Parish registers

Dating in some localities from the mid-16th century, parish registers list baptisms, marriages and burials occurring in churches and chapels. The names of those concerned are given, as well as where they lived and the dates the ceremonies took place. Additional detail often appears over time. Thus from 1813, and sometimes earlier, baptism entries give fathers' occupations and burial entries the age at death. Supposed causes of death are sometimes given, too, as are bridegrooms' occupations in marriage registers.[25]

24 J. Halewood, 'Using school log books – Bishop Graham Memorial Ragged School, Chester', *Primary History*, 24 (January, 2000), pp.22-4. For comment on other types of source material relating to schools, including attendance registers and punishment books, along with suggestions for classroom use of the material they contain, see S. Leach, 'Teaching about my school in the past using original sources or why would I want those old books in my classroom?', *Primary History*, 73 (Summer, 2016), pp.22-5.

25 Norfolk Record Office's *Information Leaflet 45: Parish Registers* gives further details in easily-

Many parish registers have been transcribed and printed, so that pages from them can be readily photocopied for classroom use. The example shows entries for 1795. Additionally, a growing number of parish register transcriptions that form part of the *Online Parish Clerks'* project are becoming available. The project started in the South West and has spread to other counties in various parts of the country. A list of counties currently involved can be found at <http://onlineparishclerks.org.uk/>. Microfilm copies of the original parish registers can be viewed in local libraries.

William Son of Francis Leyland & Mary his Wife, Westhall, Butcher, died Decr 10th, buried 12th. Aged 1 year
Margaret Widow to the late Thomas Light of Middleton, Labourer, died Decr 11th, buried 14th. Aged 81
1795. Mary Widow to the late George Teal of Ilkley, Taylor, died March 5th, buried March 8th. Aged 89
Isabel daughter of Ann Aspinal of Austby, Spinster, died March 13th, buried March 14th
Mary Widow to the late Richard Batty of Ilkley, Millar, died May 20th, buried 23^{d}. Aged 77
John Son of John Stephenson of Ilkley & Mary his Wife, Dealer, died May 26th, buried the 28th. Aged 11
James Ramsden of Wheatley, Labourer, died June 2^{d}, buried 5th. Ag^{d} 68
Richard Vickers of Ilkley, Butcher, died June 2^{d}, buried 5th. Aged 47
Rose Wife of Thomas Hargate of Middleton, Farmer, R.C., died June 26th, buried the 28th. Aged 61
Grace Cunliffe D. of Betty Brumfitt of Burley, died Augst 11th, bur^{d} 13th. Ag^{d} 1
John Hepworth of Woodhead, ffarmer, R.C., died Octr 19th, bur^{d} 22^{d}. Agd. 62
Stephen Son of Thomas Hearfield, Burley, Labourer, died Oct. 30th, bur^{d} Novr 5. Ag^{d} 1
Mary D. of Wm Gott of Ilkley, Lab^{r}, & Sarah his Wife, died Decr 25th, bur^{d} 27th. Ag^{d} 2 y^{rs} [215]

Source: W. Cooper (ed.), *The Parish register of Ilkley, 1597-1812* (1927), p.190.

In this West Yorkshire example, the ages of death are given and the high levels of child mortality that prevailed are only too apparent. Yet, as can be seen, some people did live to an advanced age. Male occupations are also recorded, as are the dates of both death and burial.

Parish register evidence can be used to investigate a range of historical concerns at local level, especially before civil registration of births, deaths and marriages was introduced in England and Wales during 1837. These concerns include patterns of population change; the extent and causes of mortality crises; population size; and male occupational details.[26]

---

accessible form. It can be seen at <http://www.archives.norfolk.gov.uk/view/NCC098531>.

26 Robert Alfano has shown how children in his year 8 class used annual baptism, burial and marriage totals keyed into a spreadsheet to determine population growth during the 18th century at Wellington in Somerset. See R. Alfano, 'Databases, spreadsheets and historical enquiry at key stage 3', *Teaching History*, 101 (November, 2000), pp.45-7. See also

Diaries, autobiographies and letters

These types of source record a great deal about local life in the past and, in common with parish registers, they have often been transcribed and published. They can give children useful details about everyday events, including the food people ate, the clothes they wore, the weather they experienced and the work in which they were engaged. The detail they provide varies considerably, however, and those that are indexed will clearly be easier to use in finding material that relates to a chosen theme.

The following extract illustrates the type of uses these sources can have. It is taken from the diary of Robert Sharp, a schoolmaster who lived at South Cave, to the west of Hull in East Yorkshire, during the early decades of the 19th century.[27]

> At west end last night very rainy and Stormy, it was uncommonly dark when I came back, I slipped off the road into a Spring besides Thurnham's, but without injury except getting wet on one of my feet and the Stocking dirtied on the other.

One point for children to appreciate is that rural roads were unlit at night during Sharp's lifetime, so that walking along them could pose dangers. They might also surmise that the road surface was muddy and slippery from the recent rain. Also, because he dirtied one of his stockings when he slipped, he was probably wearing knee-breeches rather than full-length trousers. Perhaps he was something of a traditionalist as far as dress was concerned, since trousers were becoming more fashionable for men's wear at the time he wrote.

Obtaining written source material

Libraries may prove to be the most fruitful starting point to begin reviewing and collecting written source material for local history studies and a visit to examine the material available and to talk with library staff is likely to be highly productive. However, much useful information can be gleaned from searches in local library catalogues, which can be consulted online. Photocopies of various types of source material held in library collections can usually be made.

Record offices under the control of local authorities can be found throughout the country, with at least one per county. They are mainly concerned with manuscript sources, though they also make other types of material available, including local maps. Diana Knapp relates how she used copies of letters, photographs and other family documents supplied by East Sussex Record Office to enable her class to tell the story of a family that lived in the school neighbourhood.[28] The education provision that record offices make available varies, but contacts from teachers are

---

H. Glendinning and G. Timmins, 'Population history with juniors: using parish registers', *Teaching History*, 36 (June, 1983), pp.16-18. This article describes classroom investigation into family mortality using parish register entries for Colne and Kirkham in Lancashire.

27 J. E. Crowther and P. A. Crowther, *The Diary of Robert Sharp of South Cave: Life in a Yorkshire Village, 1812-1837* (Oxford University Press, 1997), p.120.

28 D. Knapp, 'A good place for an investigation: using sources to develop a local history project', *Primary History*, 16 (June, 1997), pp.4-6. The article also gives useful advice on organising children into groups to undertake their investigations of the sources.

welcomed.[29]

In approaching organisations to obtain written source material, several considerations arise.

- Booking an appointment to discuss requirements and to view possible source material is usually helpful to potential resource providers. Being forewarned, they may be able to have material waiting to be viewed on arrival. Trying to avoid their busier times should facilitate more productive contacts.
- Being as explicit as possible about the theme or themes that are of interest will help providers to meet requirements more effectively. They may be able to unearth material from sources that are unfamiliar.
- Some of the source material required may only be available to view in the form of microfilm copies. It is often possible to have hard copies made, however. Alternatively, selective copying by hand might be feasible.
- Whilst children should use a range of primary sources, the quantity required need not be large. Indeed, the most effective local history teaching is likely to be achieved by using a limited amount of high-quality source material.

Conclusion

The coverage in this chapter by no means exhausts the range of written sources that might be useful in teaching local history. However, those selected have the advantage of being relatively easy to access, either online or in local libraries. They are also accessible in the sense that they are in printed form or in a handwriting style that is likely to be familiar enough for children to read, albeit with some guidance. Other sources, such as probate inventories, which list the possessions of deceased people, tend to be far less accessible. This is partly because they date from the early modern period, so the handwriting can be difficult to read and the terms they contain unfamiliar. Also, they are more likely to be kept in record offices rather than local libraries. Even so, printed transcriptions may be available and there are guides to the terminology used in them. Moreover, guidance on their use in the primary school classroom is available.[30] Other early modern records that might also be transcribed included those of manorial courts, which can prove highly revealing about aspects of daily life in early modern times and beyond. Those for Manchester, for example, give details on such matters as muzzling dogs; preventing food adulteration; coping with domestic sanitation; and maintaining water supply.[31] Historians in local universities may well be of help in obtaining source material of this type.

29 Helpful advice on using record offices to facilitate local history teaching can be found in J. Halewood, 'A treasure trove of local history – how to use your local record office', *Primary History*, 24 (January, 2000), pp.10-11; M. Mills, 'Accessing archive sources', *Primary History*, 34 (May, 2003), pp.24-6; and A. Carter, 'What your local archive service can offer to schools', *Primary History*, 70 (June, 2015), pp.40-1.

30 G. Rogers, 'The use of primary evidence in the junior school classroom', *Teaching History*, 38 (February, 1984), pp.22-5 and M. Fogg, 'The use of sixteenth/seventeenth century wills and inventories as historical sources in the primary school', *Teaching History*, 80 (June, 1995), pp.27-30.

31 Several volumes can be viewed online. For example, volume 3, which covers the period from 1618 to1641, can be seen at <https://archive.org/details/courtleetrecord05coungoog>.

Chapter 3
Non-written sources for local history

The scope for teaching local history in schools, especially in the early years, is greatly enhanced when non-written sources are taken into account. They bring opportunity to broaden the range of investigations that children can undertake, both in terms of theme and time period. They also allow investigations to be deepened, especially when combined with written evidence. In this chapter, three groups of non-written sources are identified and described. As in the previous chapter, comment is made on the value they have for teaching purposes and details are given about how they can be obtained. The chapter concludes with a section noting websites that provide non-written as well as written sources.

Classification of non-written sources

Three broad categories of non-written sources can be distinguished. These are defined in the table below and examples are given. The classification is useful in highlighting something of the extensive range of non-written source material that is available at local level and that can be drawn on for teaching purposes.

CLASSIFICATION OF NON-WRITTEN SOURCES	
Source type	*Examples*
Visual	Maps; photographs; engravings; films; paintings; postcards.
Oral testimony	Taped interviews; conversations with people; video recordings.
Physical: (a) artefacts	Household and workplace utensils; pot sherds; clothing; toys; machinery.
(b) landscape features	Houses; roads, canals and railways; farm, industrial and commercial premises; schools; churches and chapels; field boundaries; mines and quarries; gravestones; monuments.

The examples shown do no more than raise possibilities from which, according to circumstances, choices can be made. However, it is certainly feasible and perhaps desirable, to involve children in using at least some forms of visual, oral and physical evidence in their local history studies throughout the key stages.

Visual sources

Maps

The first relatively accurate and large-scale maps (often one-inch to a mile) became available for counties during the 18th and early 19th centuries, though earlier ones on smaller scales are widely available.[32] Ordnance Survey county maps were also published on the one-inch scale, beginning in the early 19th century.

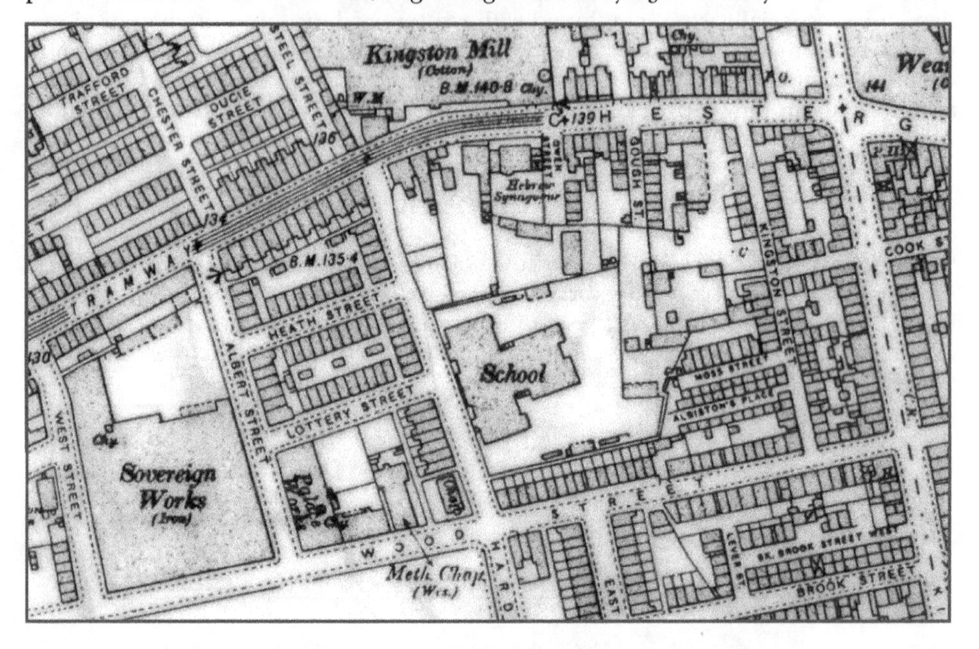

Source: 25-inch Ordnance Survey of Stockport, Cheshire, 1910, sheet X 15.

The map shows part of Stockport, Greater Manchester. The newer houses are on the west side of the map and the older ones on the east side. All the newer houses were through houses – they had both front and back doors and were two rooms deep – with several of those bordering the main road having rear extensions. They also had their own back yards separated by narrow back streets. However, some of the older houses were back-to-backs – they shared a back wall and were only one room deep. Examples are shown at Albiston's Place and Brook Street. Even with the through houses, back yard space for the older housing was shared and sometimes accessed by passageways placed at intervals along the rows. Housing standards varied considerably, therefore.

32 Details of early county maps are given in J. B. Harley, *Maps for the Local Historian* (The Standing Conference for Local History,1977), ch.6. The author points to a revolution in county map-making during the 18th century with the introduction of scientific triangulation and the adoption of the one inch to the mile scale. Most counties benefited from the revolution.

From the 1840s, the Ordnance Survey also covered whole counties on a scale of 6 inches to one mile and 25 inches to one mile. The latter are particularly useful because, as the extract below shows, they are on a large enough scale to show individual houses within rows of houses. Additionally, for some parts of the country, the Ordnance Survey published large-scale town plans at 5 feet and 10 feet to the mile.[33] The dates of publication for these maps, and of revised editions of them, vary from place to place and local library and archive websites should be consulted about availability. Copyright restrictions exist for Ordnance Survey maps less than fifty years old. Plainly, children can use maps dating from different periods to help in revealing how local towns and villages developed. Other types of printed local maps are often available that relate to particular themes, such as transport. Local librarians and archivists will advise.

Some local authorities have made available online copies of Ordnance Survey and other local maps. They include the *East Riding Archive Maps* and the *Old Maps of Lancashire* initiatives, the websites for which are <http://treasurehouse.eastriding.gov.uk/Help.aspx> and <http://www3.lancashire.gov.uk/environment/oldmap/>. The National Library of Scotland has made available online copies of Ordnance Survey and other maps for the country covering the period 1560-1964. They can be seen at <http://maps.nls.uk/index.html>. CD versions of local maps are also becoming increasingly available, whilst the Alan Godfrey reprints of old Ordnance Survey maps offer high-quality reproductions at modest cost.[34]

Photographs, engravings and paintings

Within local authority areas, libraries, museums and art galleries hold extensive collections of photographs and other types of visuals. The subject range is wide. However, cost and copyright considerations need to be borne in mind when planning to use them for teaching purposes and advice should be sought. Additionally, numerous visual sources can be found in the secondary works on local history, especially those published during the last few decades. And some local history books are based on past and present depictions of outdoor scenes. Helpful comment on the content and significance of the images is given, though this is often limited. In older local histories, visual images, especially engravings of buildings and street scenes, can frequently be found; they may well be out of copyright and cheap to reproduce.[35] In many instances, library online cataloguing extends to holdings of visual images, which can be searched and viewed using key words.[36]

33 Guidance on the Ordnance Survey and other maps useful for local history teaching can be found, for example, in B. P. Hindle, *Maps for Local History* (Batsford,1988). For Ordnance Survey maps alone, see R. Oliver, *Ordnance Survey Maps: A Concise Guide for Historians* (The Charles Close Society, 1993).

34 Most of the Godfrey edition maps are reproductions of 25-inch to the mile OS maps. They are reprinted on a scale of about 14 inches to the mile. The series also includes copies of the 1840s 5 feet to the mile maps for Liverpool and Manchester.

35 They tend to give positive images and are highly selective with regard to locality.

36 For guidance on finding local photographs, along with some remarkable examples, see G. Oliver, *Photographs and Local History* (Batsford,1989). The varying types of school photographs that can be obtained, along with ideas for their use in the classroom, can be found in S. Purkis, *A Teacher's Guide to Using School Buildings* (English Heritage, 1993), pp.24-7.

Writing in the early 1980s, Robert Unwin discussed the ways in which children can take their own local photographs as part of their historical studies. He points to the benefits that can arise with regard to children appreciating photographic techniques and presenting the results of their investigations. He also notes that their photographs bring advantage by contributing to the historical record.[37] Given the development of digital photography and the availability of computer software to display and manipulate visual images, much substance is added to his comments. In fact, creating visual images will help to develop an appreciation of their limitations as historical sources, especially because of the bias and distortions that the photographer can bring to bear.[38] Thus, quite a different impression of a local street scene can be created if a photograph is taken on a sunny day rather than a rainy day or on a Sunday rather than a market day.

Local aerial photographs dating from between 1919 and 1953 that form part of the *Britain From Above* archive can be viewed on line at <http://www.britainfromabove.org.uk/>. Many of the images show parts of built-up areas, with key features being identified.

Films

The British Film Institute has made available numerous local film clips that can be viewed online. One group, entitled *The Big Smoke: London on Film*, contains clips going back to Edwardian times. Remarkable street scenes, with numerous horse-drawn vehicles, including omnibuses and Hansom cabs, can be seen. The clips can be viewed at <https://www.youtube.com/playlist?list=PL2189B4FCA011C2A1>. Other historical film clips relating to different parts of the country, which can be selected from a map, are available in the Institute's *Britain on Film* section at <http://player.bfi.org.uk/britain-on-film/>.[39]

Regional film archives also make online provision. Amongst them is *Scottish Screen Archive*, which contains an extensive collection relating to various parts of Scotland. It includes, for example, a 1945 film depicting everyday life at the crofting community of Achriesgill in Sutherland. Sheep shearing by hand and cutting and stacking peat are two of the aspects shown. The archive, which can be searched by place, subject and decade, is at <http://ssa.nls.uk/>. Other regional film archives that make similar provision are the *East Anglian Film Archive*, the *North West Film Archive* and the *Yorkshire Film Archive*.

Oral testimony

Oral testimony that can be used in local history teaching can also be found online. It includes the extensive archive that comprises the BBC's *Millennium Memory Bank*. Compiled during the closing weeks of the millennium, this archive

37 R. Unwin, *The Visual Dimension in the Study and Teaching of History* (Historical Association Teaching History Series, 49, 1981), pp.21-2.

38 For a discussion on these matters, see S. T. Miller, 'The value of photographs as historical evidence', *The Local Historian*, 15 (1983), pp.468-73.

39 The British Film Institute has also produced a teachers' guide to using film and television with three- to eleven-year-olds. The guide is entitled *Look Again!* and can be downloaded at <http://old.bfi.org.uk/education/teaching/lookagain/>.

centres on the everyday experiences of people throughout Britain and the changes they perceived to have taken place within their communities. Respondents were drawn from diverse ethnic and socio-economic backgrounds; 56 per cent of them were male; and they ranged in age from five to 107 years. Respondents can be found by county and a synopsis is given of the issues on which the respondents comment. In the case of Cornwall, for example, there are six respondents, their interviews lasting between about 4.5 and 9.5 minutes. One respondent, living at St. Kew, deliberates on the migration of people into Cornwall during his lifetime, noting the advantages and disadvantages he perceives to have arisen. For Kent, to take another example, there are twelve respondents, one of whom, from Gillingham, talks about his early schooldays during the 1960s. The site can be visited at <http://sounds.bl.uk/Accents-and-dialects/Millenium-memory-bank>.

At regional level, the East Midlands Oral History Archive makes provision for teachers. The schools' section of the archive's website contains details of a project entitled the *Oral History of Toys and Games.* A CD of extracts from the project interviews can be purchased. However, some of the extracts, along with transcriptions, can be listened to online. Summaries of all the extracts, as well as an accompanying pack for teachers, can be freely downloaded. Ideas for classroom activities are given, along with information sheets concerned with conducting oral history interviews. The site also features an exhibition entitled *Leicestershire & Rutland Remember the First World War.* Again, several extracts from the interviews are available. Themes covered include life on the home front. The site is at <https://www.le.ac.uk/emoha/>.

At county level, the *Somerset Voices Oral History Archive* is noteworthy. The archive contains over 500 recordings that depict aspects of everyday life in Somerset during the twentieth century. Short audio-clips with transcriptions are featured, along with photographs of the respondents or of the theme with which they are dealing. The site navigation enables the respondents to be identified by the place they refer to and the subject matter they cover. The complete recordings can be heard at the Somerset Record Office in Taunton or the Somerset Rural Life Museum at Glastonbury. The extracts cover a varied range of topics, including domestic life, agricultural practices and life during World War II. The archive is at <http://www.somersetvoices.org.uk/>.

Many local people are willing to provide oral testimony about their past experiences. This type of evidence is commonly obtained by means of taped interviews and succinct guidance on undertaking them can be found in the BBC's *A Guide to Oral History*. Discussion in the guide is arranged under the following headings:

- Identify a subject or theme
- Choose a location and recording equipment
- Prepare open interview questions
- Be sensitive, as the process can be emotional
- Remember an interview is just one person's opinion

The guide can be found at <http://downloads.bbc.co.uk/history/handsonhistory/a_guide_to_oral_history.pdf>.

Where common questions are asked, children will obtain evidence that will help them to generalise, albeit in a guarded way. To keep their task manageable, only a few respondents need be involved. The number of questions might also be limited to a dozen or so, but with children being encouraged to ask supplementary questions when they feel that the respondent has more to say on some aspect of the interview.

An alternative approach to taping conversations is to use question sheets that, for the most part, are designed to elicit specific responses. Examples, along with the underpinning rationale, are given in chapter 8.

Physical evidence

Artefacts

Artefacts that children can use as part of their local history investigations may be obtained in various ways. Items from museum collections are commonly utilised, either on site or through loans to schools. As noted in chapter 4, parents and others associated with schools might also make provision, as might local archaeology societies. A few, well-chosen objects that help to develop understanding of the topic in hand will suffice. Further comments on their classroom use are given in chapter 10.[40]

Another way of obtaining artefacts has been advocated by Peter Hammond. He points out that field walking can produce fragments of artefacts – pottery, bones, clay pipes, and so on – that are suitable for classroom use. Many of these fragments became part of the household rubbish disposed of in Victorian privies, details of which are given in chapter 9. The contents of these privies were often emptied out on farm land, so that the fragments became widely scattered.[41] Fragments of this type can also emerge when gardens are being cultivated. Additionally, attic storage areas can prove to be a fruitful source of artefacts for classroom use.

Landscape features

As is apparent from the table at the outset of this chapter, landscape history is broadly based. In fact, W. G. Hoskins, the doyen of English landscape history, has remarked that the sub-discipline is concerned 'with everything that has altered the natural landscape'. He has noted, too, that studying landscape history involves combining evidence derived from fieldwork with that from documentary sources.[42] School buildings, along with buildings that can be viewed from the school grounds, provide one opportunity for children to undertake field investigation. Worksheets can be prepared to guide them in observing and recording the main features of the buildings. In addition to questions, the worksheets might contain partly-completed sketches of the buildings, which the children can complete on site. The evidence derived might be used for comparative purposes, exploring, say, the

40 Discussion of the varied range of objects relating to school life can be found in Purkis, *Teacher's Guide*, pp.28-31.

41 P. Hammond, 'A load of rubbish: using Victorian throwaways in the classroom', *Primary History*, 36 (Spring, 2004), pp.12-15.

42 W. G. Hoskins, *The Making of the English Landscape* (Penguin reprint, 1973), pp.14-15.

changing design characteristics of schools since Victorian times.[43] The same type of approaches can be adopted in viewing other local sites.

Where direct investigation of sites beyond the school grounds proves difficult to organise, taking photographs of the built environment for classroom use may be possible; children will still be making use of physical evidence, albeit indirectly, and will help to create a record of it. In fact, this approach enables them to study physical evidence taken from several sites, not all of which they would be able to visit, at least as a class group. Fuller use can therefore be made of the range of physical evidence that is germane to their studies. In advocating this approach, Gordon Guest also suggests that a survey might be undertaken of the type of dwellings in which class members and their relatives live.[44]

Field evidence can bring advantage by extending the scope of children's local history investigations. With regard to Victorian terraced houses, for instance, they can find out about changes in the nature of the building materials used, and the ways in which they were used, as the period progressed. They might also find evidence about the storage of coal, either in cellars or back-yard buildings; the number and location of fireplaces - and hence the internal layout of the houses - by studying chimney pot provision; and the removal of excreta and ashes via ground-floor openings in rear yard walls. These matters are further considered in chapter 9, along with opportunities that arise for investigating other features of the built environment, including roads, canals and railways; churches and churchyards; and gravestones and war memorials.

The *Heritage Explorer* section of the Historic England website contains thousands of images relating to the built environment that can be searched and downloaded into worksheets and presentations. Coverage is nationwide and includes numerous photographs of historic sites and buildings that span the ages, along with aerial views of localities and scenes of daily life. The site also offers detailed advice on how the images can be used in the classroom at each key stage. The images are arranged in themes, which are listed, each containing a selection of the images available. These themes include castles, road transport, Edwardian life, the seaside; and past shopping. The site can be viewed at <http://www.heritageexplorer.org.uk>.

Other online sources

In this and the preceding chapter, attention has been drawn to websites that deal solely or mainly with a particular type of primary source that has value in teaching local history. However, there are other websites that offer several types of primary material that can be used for this purpose, both in written and non-written forms. They include:

- *From Weaver to Web* is an online archive relating to the history of Calderdale in West Yorkshire. A varied range of primary source material, mostly visual, is reproduced and the themes to which it relates include Halifax theatres and Calderdale architecture. The resources can be viewed at <http://www.calderdale.gov.uk/wtw/>.

43 Developments in school buildings are considered in Purkis, *Teacher's Guide*, pp.4-9.

44 G. Guest, 'Looking at buildings as a source for developing historical enquiries', *Primary History*, 28 (May, 2001), pp.5-17.

- The *Education* component of The National Archives website, which is divided into broad time periods, contains sections that deal with local history. For instance, coverage of the early modern period includes resources on the Great Fire of London; the Second World War section has resources on evacuation to Shropshire; the Industry and Empire 1750 – 1850 section includes resources on the Rebecca Riots in South Wales; and the medieval section contains resources on the town of Chertsey in Surrey. Visit the site at <http://www.nationalarchives.gov.uk/education/>.
- The *Primary Sources* website, noted above in the section on school log books, contains a range of other primary source material relating to counties in North-east England. Themes covered include: *The impact of World War II on the lives of children* (Middlesbrough); *Britain since 1948* (Newcastle); and *The Coming of the Railway* (Berwick). Lesson plans are also provided. The resources on the website are designed to facilitate literacy and numeracy teaching at primary level. The site is at <http://www.primarysources.org.uk/>.
- The Huskar colliery disaster is one amongst those recorded on the *Pitwork* website, which deals with various aspects of coal mining history in Britain. This disaster, which occurred at Silkstone, near Barnsley in Yorkshire, provides an intriguing story about why only children died, as well as giving both physical and documentary evidence that children can combine to investigate what happened. The site can be viewed at <http://www.dmm.org.uk/pitwork/html/daz.htm>.
- The *My Learning* website contains free learning resources provided by arts, cultural and heritage organisations, including visual material and background texts. Some local history themes are covered, mainly relating to the north of England. Amongst them are *Leeds in World War II* and *Bradford's Industrial Revolution*. Several of the history units form component parts of a World War I centenary project called *Preston Remembers*. The website is at <http://www.mylearning.org/>.[45]
- Newman University's *Local History* website contains a varied range of primary sources from different time periods relating to the history of Birmingham and the West Midlands, including a set of World War II photographs. They can be seen at <http://www.newmanlocalhistory.org.uk/>.
- The BBC *WW2 People's War* website is an archive of World War II stories and photographs contributed by members of the public. It contains an astonishing 47,000 stories, which cover a varied range of themes, along with 15,000 images, which include wartime scenes. People throughout Britain have made contributions and the archive can be searched by locality. The site also contains a learning zone section, which provides resources for teachers. View the site at <http://www.bbc.co.uk/ww2peopleswar/>.
- *History House* contains various transcriptions of primary sources relating to the history of Essex. Resources for particular towns and villages can be searched. For Kelvedon Hatch, to take one example, there are transcriptions of school log books, census returns and trade directories. The log book entries date from 1879-84 and 1884-97 and are more detailed than is commonly the case. They provide some graphic and revealing accounts both of events that occurred and the attitudes that underpinned them. There are also photographs of some of the pupils and teachers. The site is at <http://www.historyhouse.co.uk/index.html>.

45 For further information about the website, see A. Hellon and E. Amis-Hughes, 'My learning: bringing history to life', *Primary History*, 61 (Summer, 2012), pp.17-19.

Conclusion

When this and the previous chapter are considered as a whole, it becomes quite apparent that a remarkably wide range of source material is available to support learning and teaching in local history. And this is so with regard to each key stage and to all localities in the country. Of course, some localities are better served than others as far as particular types of evidence are concerned, a point that is perhaps best made when that drawn from the built environment is considered. Yet in places that lack examples of, say, early modern timber-framed houses or the remains of a medieval castle, the source material available is still more than adequate to allow a high degree of choice to be made in the local history investigations that children can undertake.

Chapter 4
Planning considerations

Even in primary and secondary schools that follow the National Curriculum, there is no constraint regarding time period or theme to which a local history study can relate. A lack of prescription is certainly to be welcomed because of the freedom it brings to exercise professional judgement and to follow up particular interests of teacher and taught. Yet careful planning of classroom activities is required to ensure that worthwhile learning opportunities are created. The purpose of this chapter is to consider approaches that can be adopted in meeting this need. The emphasis is on planning activities that involve children in using primary sources to investigate themes that are clearly defined and that have significance in promoting their understanding of the nature of history as an academic discipline. Consideration is given to theme selection, choice of theme content, progression matters and preparing classroom resources.

Theme selection

In deciding on the overall theme for a local history study, a number of issues arise. To the fore amongst them is whether or not appropriate source material can be made available for children to use in the classroom. One consideration here is that more source material will be available at local level for themes situated in the more recent past than in earlier times. Thus for themes dealing with the Victorian period or later, photographic evidence is available, whilst for post-Second World War themes children can draw directly on oral testimony. And for twentieth century themes in general, filmic evidence can be added to the mix. Choosing a modern local history theme also allows primary schools that follow the National Curriculum to make additional provision in the post-Norman Conquest period.

To make these points is not to argue that local history themes relating to the pre-Victorian period should be avoided. On the contrary, they can offer rich opportunities, perhaps enabling aspects of major national events, such as the English Civil War, to be investigated in some depth. Moreover, if physical remains such as a castle, monastery or manor house can be accessed in the locality, advantage will arise from children being able to make use of the historical evidence they provide. There is also the consideration that those secondary schools following the National Curriculum may have opportunity to extend the limited excursions they are allowed to make into the pre-Norman era.

A further matter to address concerning theme selection relates to types of history. A local history study might well be used to provide greater balance in a school history curriculum by focusing on types of history that are not well represented elsewhere. Women's history, including women as political activists at local level, might be an example.[46] So, too, might children's history, engagement with which could focus on school and work dimensions, drawing on evidence from such sources as school log books, parliamentary enquiries and census enumerators' schedules.

Theme selection in local history might also extend to cross-curricular links. To take one instance, as noted in chapter 1, opportunities abound for children to engage with numeracy. Possibilities include using printed census data to create graphs showing local population change, perhaps using spreadsheet facilities, and extracting census schedule data to produce graphs of the age and gender of Victorian scholars. In fact, census schedule data can be used in several ways, including the analysis of local occupational distributions in order to find the proportions of people falling into the standard primary, construction, secondary and tertiary occupational categories.[47] The results obtained from exercises of this type are not ends in themselves, the point being that children can use simple numerical techniques to provide the basis on which historical interpretation can be made. Examples are given in chapters 6 and 8.

National Curriculum local history themes

Three examples of local history themes that might be addressed appear in early National Curriculum documentation. They were intended to support provision at key stage 2, but could equally well apply at key stage 3.[48]

People on the move

This is seen in the documentation as a long-period study that concerns movement of people to and from local communities as well as within them. It is suggested that children might study the effects of people moving on the language, culture, way of life and the physical environment of the locality. The exercise on children's forenames in chapter 6 links with this theme. In considering why population movements occurred, the documentation suggests that links could be made with other history study units, including that dealing with the invasion and settlement by Romans, Anglo-Saxons and Vikings. With regard to causes of population movements, mention is made of the search for land, trade and raw materials.[49]

46 For discussion on the value and opportunities that local history sources, especially local newspapers, can have in teaching women's history, see D. Welbourne, 'Deconstruction to reconstruction: an approach to women's history through local history', *Teaching History*, 59 (April, 1990), pp.16-22. Details of local suffragettes in various parts of the country can be found online at <http://localsuffragettes.wikispaces.com/>.

47 Primary activity is concerned with mining and quarrying, agriculture and fishing; secondary activity with manufacturing, including light and heavy industries; and tertiary activity with services of various types, including transport, wholesale and retail trade, professional work and domestic service. Labourers are included in the service sector. Construction, which includes people described as masons, bricklayers and so on, usually constitutes a very small proportion of any local workforce.

48 National Curriculum Council, 'Non-statutory guidance for history', Department of Education and Science, *History in the National Curriculum (England)*, HMSO, 1991, pp.F7–F9.

49 The Geographical Association website contains a short contextual article entitled *A History of Migration*. It deals with the reasons for migrants coming into Britain, noting the invaders of the first millennium and Europeans fleeing from religious persecution during the Reformation, thereby giving examples of pull and push factors. It also notes the much greater volume of post-

Suggested sources for children to use are census returns, gravestones, school registers, trade directories and local newspapers.

Of these sources, census enumerators' schedules can certainly be used to examine local migration patterns during the Victorian era, making use of information in the birth place column. Children could take a sample for a locality, dividing people according to whether they were born in the locality, in neighbouring localities or from more distant parts.[50] They might test the hypothesis that most migration was from a short distance. They might also examine the age and gender of migrants. Printed census returns also give birth-place details for counties, census districts and principal towns and cities. For example, they reveal that 56 per cent of Glasgow's population in 1851 were immigrants, of whom virtually a third came from Ireland.[51] 'Push' factors associated with the Irish potato famine of the 1840s, along with 'pull' factors relating to the job opportunities that the mainland cities closest to Ireland could offer, would both have influenced this situation.

As to more recent population movements, local authority websites can be helpful. So, too, can Oxford University's *Migration Observatory*. A section of its website gives graphs that deal with numbers and percentages of migrants recorded in the 2011 census at regional and sub-regional levels. [52] The website is at <http://www.migrationobservatory.ox.ac.uk/projects/migration-in-the-census>.

War on the home front, 1939-45

For this short-period study, the documentation suggests studying the effects of World War II on women, men and children from different backgrounds, covering such topics as air-raids and air-raid precautions, evacuation, rationing, diet and changes in jobs. Using oral testimony is suggested, along with written and visual sources, not all of them local.

In terms of historical understanding, children might consider the nature and extent of the disruption that occurred to everyday life and how people managed to cope with the difficult and often tragic situations they encountered. The extensive resources available on the BBC's *WW2 People's War* website, noted in chapter 3, will help with resourcing a unit of this type. So, too, will extracts from contemporary local newspapers, examples of which are given in Chapter 2. The theme is

---

World War II immigration that arose and the wider geographical area from which migrants came to seek work, including Europe, the West Indies and the Indian sub-continent. The article can be seen at <http://www.geography.org.uk/search.asp?searchfor=migration&searchin=all>. Context is also provided in K. Hann, 'Migration: the search for a better life', *Primary History*, 37 (Summer, 2004), pp.6-9. For further details and analysis of post-World War II immigration trends, see Office for National Statistics, *Immigration Patterns of Non-UK Born Populations in England and Wales in 2011* (December, 2013). The document can be viewed at <http://www.ons.gov.uk/ons/dcp171776_346219.pdf>.

50 The sample might be drawn from one or more enumeration districts within a town, or perhaps part of an enumeration district. Local migrants occurring within the sample might be defined as those from enumeration districts surrounding the town.

51 *Census of Great Britain, 1851, Population Tables II, Vol. II, Scotland*, p.1041.

52 The 2001 and 2011 immigrant figures for localities can also as be seen on the website of the Office for National Statistics: Neighbourhood Statistics at <http://www.neighbourhood.statistics.gov.uk/dissemination/>.

exemplified in the 'Bristol Blitz Experience', an activity undertaken by Dean Smart with his year 9 children. The exercise involved the children in role play, which provided a stimulus to writing and research. They used a range of artefacts, many of which were donated by local people, as well as a purpose-made Anderson shelter.[53] The theme might also be addressed in relation to the First World War, of course, perhaps with comparisons being made. The resources provided by the British Association for Local History, which are outlined in the secondary sources section of chapter 2, will help in this respect.

Domestic life in the local area in Victorian times

Topics suggested are household structure, domestic servants, daily routines, diet, education, toys and games. The local sources mentioned are census returns, recipes, photographs, memoirs and artefacts. Where possible, visits to local museums and houses are advocated.

The household structure theme could lead to a consideration of the contrasting lifestyles led by families at different levels of society, making use of evidence drawn from local large-scale Ordnance Survey maps, public health reports, census enumerators' schedules and surviving houses. A mid-19th century comparison might be made between large (middle-class) and small (working-class) terraced houses situated close to town centres. A late-19th century comparison might be made between the former type of house and the detached and semi-detached houses built for the well-to-do in newly-formed residential suburbs. Associated themes could also be developed. One could be about the degree of improvement made to the houses of ordinary families in the locality during Victorian times, not least with regard to sanitary provision. This matter is considered in Chapter 9. Another, focusing on the same period, could examine why residential suburbs developed for well-to-do families during Victorian times. The lack of town centre space to build large houses for rising numbers of middle-class families and the growing demands made on this space by expanding commercial activity, both wholesale and retail, could be noted. Mention could also be made of the attractions of suburban living, including the provision of healthier and more private environments than those within towns.

A contextualising, long-period theme involving considerations of continuity and change might deal with the rise of the mechanised home. Comparisons might be made between the present day, drawing on children's own experiences; the 1950s, making use of oral testimony, perhaps derived along the lines suggested in chapter 8; and the late Victorian era, using artefacts (or photographs of them) and illustrations contained in contemporary advertisements. Much of the evidence used can be generated within, and relate to, a particular locality. Aspects covered could include developments in heating (open fires giving way to central heating); lighting (electric lights replacing candles, oil lamps and gas lighting); cooking (open fires and kitchen ranges being replaced by gas cookers and electric cookers, including microwave ovens); cleaning clothes (hand washing being superseded by washing machines of various types); and house cleaning (the rise of vacuum cleaners). Advances in domestic sanitation can also be included. In undertaking such a study, children can consider the nature of change and the degree to which

53 See D. Smart, '"Balloons over Barton Hill": recreating the Bristol Blitz using artefacts and role play', *Primary History*, 31 (Spring, 2002), pp.18-21.

labour saving has occurred; households vary with regard to how much they are mechanised. Children might also gain some idea of the timing and causes of innovation and of the important role that the rise of public utilities has played in improving housing quality.

Advertisements in local trade directories and, in some localities, illustrated guides, can prove helpful in providing evidence on the household equipment that was available during and beyond Victorian times. Examples from the Victorian period are given in Appendix 1.

Other local history themes

The following themes are amongst others that offer excellent learning and teaching possibilities in local history and that can be undertaken in any locality.[54]

Urban and rural development

Children's investigations into town and village history can deal with settlements as a whole or in part and can cover varying time periods. The nature, pace and extent of development can be studied, as well as the causes and impact of change. Population figures and occupational details taken from national censuses and parish register entries, along with evidence derived from maps, trade directories and the built environment will provide much of the material required. The growth of industry and trade in towns could deal with particular sectors over short periods of time, but might also chart long-term developments over, say the last 200 years.[55] The aim might be to help children to appreciate the changing importance at local level of primary, secondary and tertiary activity. Discussion might take place on the impact of the changes that have occurred and views sought on whether or not they have proved advantageous.

For industrial towns, contextualisation might be brought in by discussion of similarities and differences in the type of industries that developed, bearing in mind that all are also centres of commerce. For villages, the discussion might distinguish between pastoral, arable and industrial economies. Change over time analysis will also bring context, especially if related to changes that have occurred nationally, not least the move towards high dependence on service industries.

Developments in transport

Emphasis might be on transport developments in more recent times, with children perhaps making particular use of oral testimony to determine how travelling for local people has changed during the post-World War II era. Consideration of the impact of car and air travel might feature, addressing both the advantages and

---

54 For other possibilities than those mentioned here, see T. Lomas (ed.), 'Some teaching and learning strategies: planning and teaching local history', *Primary History*, 25 (June, 2000), pp.14-17.

55 For examples focusing on major industries at Prescot in Merseyside and Eastleigh in Hampshire see R. Knights, 'Developing a local history project based on a local industry', *Primary History*, 39 (Spring, 2005), pp.32-3 and S. Herrity, 'Enquiry into Eastleigh's industrial past', *Teaching History*, 134 (Spring, 2009), pp.20-2.

disadvantages that have arisen at local level. Local transport changes occurring during the 18th and 19th centuries, aspects of which are further considered in chapters 6 and 9, could equally well be addressed, leading children to investigate road, canal and railway development. Matters examined might include the methods of construction used and the environmental and social impacts arising.[56] A longer-term approach could also be taken, centring on the changing speed and comfort of local travel since, say, the 18th century.

Children at work

Using evidence derived from parliamentary enquires and census enumerators' schedules, children could investigate the various types of work in which local children were engaged during the Victorian period. Their counterparts listed as scholars in the census schedules, or not being given as having occupations, could also be counted and frequency distributions compiled. They could also investigate the age and gender of child workers, drawing comparisons between the standard 0-4, 5-9 and 10-14 age groups.[57]

Context for locally-based investigations on this theme could be provided in various ways. Comparisons could be made between the mid- and late Victorian periods within a locality in order to examine the impact that compulsory education had on child labour. Point in time comparisons might also be made between localities in industrial and agricultural regions, enabling the diversity of children's work experience to be appreciated. The issue of present-day child labour, and the exploitation arising, might also be addressed.[58]

School life

In common with that on child labour, this theme has the advantage of dealing with children's history; it enables children to draw on their own experiences in making comparisons with those of scholars in the past. The theme is considered further in the following chapter, where the types of exercise that could be included within it are presented.

Choosing the content of themes

Having decided on the theme for a local history study unit, the problem arises of determining the content to include. One way forward is to think about the sources of evidence relating to the theme that might be available for classroom use. Thus, for the theme of local school life in the past, possibilities might be:

56 For discussion of teaching resources, themes and approaches concerning local railways, see T. Lomas, 'A Local history investigation at key stage 2', *Primary History*, 75 (Spring 2017), pp.22-6.

57 An example of this type of exercise can be seen on the website of the British Association for Local History at <http://www.balh.org.uk/education/classroom-exercises>. For a case study from South Wales making use of these sources, see L. M. Davies and J. A. H. Evans, 'Tales from the ironworks in Blaenavon: the Industrial Revolution and the Children's Employment Act of 1842', *Primary History*, 31 (Spring, 2002), pp.31-6.

58 H. Claire, 'Planning for diversity in the key stage 2 history curriculum: the Victorians', *Primary History*, 28 (May, 2001), pp.8-9.

- Museum artefacts, such as desks, writing slates, blackboard rubbers, inkwells, copy books, and so on.
- Contemporary illustrations, including school photographs in local library collections and in school archives, along with plans of schools.
- The school buildings, as well as photographs of other local schools built during different time periods, so that comparisons can be made.
- Brief extracts from contemporary writings, especially school log books.
- Copies of large-scale Ordnance Survey maps from the Victorian period onwards, particularly those on the six, twenty-five and sixty inch to the mile scales, to show local schools and their surroundings.
- Oral testimony from local people about their days at school, perhaps obtained directly or by using short extracts from existing recordings or transcripts.
- Details of local schools and schooling in the past mentioned in histories of the locality.

Secure in the knowledge that a range of appropriate source material is likely to be available, the next stage is to formulate key questions that the children might address. In this way, content ideas will emerge, along with thoughts about the sort of historical understanding that the children might acquire and which types of source material they might need to use. The children could be involved in the process, drawing on their own experience of school life. Class discussion on what the children think school life was like in the past might be undertaken, leading to consideration of how they could go about testing their ideas. At this stage, perhaps, brief extracts from school log books could be read out to provide an introduction and to engage interest. These extracts need not be from a local school log book, so that the question could be raised about whether the events recounted would have been similar in the children's locality or not. Context is thereby provided.

Examples of key questions relating to the schooling theme, along with the content ideas to which they give rise, are noted below. Other possibilities might be added. Reflection is needed on which sources can shed light on the questions raised, bearing in mind that some sources might prove easier to obtain than others. There is also the matter of what time period to choose. The late Victorian era would certainly enable all of the sources listed above to be tapped, including oral testimony that has been left from that time. But much could also be gained from a local theme about school life in the 1950s, which would enable children to make direct use of oral testimony. In either case, children would have opportunity to draw comparisons with their own school experiences. In so doing, they could be encouraged to think about why change has occurred, maybe considering technological advance (including the provision of computers) and changing ideas about teaching (group work versus whole class instruction). In other words, children could be led to discover the nature of change and to discuss the reasons why change has taken place. They could also consider the continuities that are evident, including the importance that is still attached to numeracy and literacy teaching.

Other local history themes can be treated in the same manner, the idea being to adopt a broad-brush approach so that a range of possibilities emerges from which a final selection can be made. The key questions and content ideas need refining to form distinct historical themes for children to address. Those incorporating the above deliberations might be:

Key questions	Content ideas
What lessons did children have in the past?	The dominance of the three Rs; boys' and girls' subjects.
What were the classrooms like in the past?	Fixed seats; fireplaces; tall and high windows; gas lighting.
What were the rest of the school premises like?	School playgrounds and outside toilets.
How was the school day organised?	Making time available for children to go home for dinner; playtimes; holidays.
How old were the scholars?	Issue of whether girls left school at an earlier age than boys.
Were the scholars regular and punctual attendees?	School attendance policy and sanctions.
How did the teachers teach and how strict were they?	Didactic methods and use of corporal punishment.

- The curriculum
- The classroom
- The scholars
- The teachers
- The school premises
- Playground games

Not all these themes need be taught, nor all of them taught in depth. Much will depend on the time available, on the age and ability of the children and on whether the resources available will be sufficient. In practice, much can be achieved and time saved by using a limited range of source material that can be easily accessed.

Preparing classroom resources

Having located a suitable selection of locally-available source material in relation to the chosen themes, issues arise with regard to how it can best be used for teaching purposes. In some instances, as with local museum exhibits or the site of a water-powered mill, it may be necessary for children to use sources away from the classroom. Indeed, if local excursions can be arranged, on-site work may prove invaluable, enabling children to use the physical evidence directly as part of their investigations. For the most part though, the available source material will be required for classroom use and will need to be made available in a form that children of varying ages and abilities can use effectively. This consideration raises several issues.

Transcribing source material

Transcribing is likely to be required where the handwriting in manuscript sources is considered too difficult for children to decipher or where the quality of reproduction proves inadequate. However, a copy of the source may still be worth showing to children so that they can appreciate the type of difficulties that arise in reading manuscript material. Indeed, comparing an original with a transcription can prove instructive for children, not least in demonstrating how letter formation and spelling have changed with time. Maybe children might try their hand at a small amount of transcribing. Where they have difficulty with particular words, taking a letter-by-letter approach can be helpful, looking at the form the letters take in words that can be determined and bearing in mind that the spelling might not be as expected.

Editing source material

The use of lengthy primary documents, including transcriptions of oral testimony, can prove tedious and off-putting for children, so that vigorous editing may be required. For instance, a few brief and well-chosen extracts from a local public health report will be enough to give children a reasonable impression of the insanitary living conditions that could occur locally in early Victorian times. Indeed, a useful exercise can be undertaken by asking children to read the extracts, to consider whether they think the town or village concerned was a healthy place to live or not at that time and to state why they conclude as they do. Discussion might follow on the difficulty of generalising from a limited amount of evidence, especially since the report from which the extracts are taken probably highlights the worst instances and does not give an overview. The same type of approach can be adopted in using oral testimony.

Using physical evidence

If field trips are difficult to organise, or if features of the built environment that can be seen from the school grounds offer too few learning opportunities, photographs could be taken so that children can use physical evidence in the classroom. This approach has the advantage of allowing particularly good examples to be selected in order to address key points. Thus to help in considering different social levels in late Victorian society, photographs could be taken of local terraced houses built at that time for ordinary families and local suburban villas built for the better off. Care is needed in making the comparison because many ordinary families would still be living in older properties with inferior facilities to those dating from late Victorian times. With regard to the Victorian schooling theme, photographs might be taken of modern and Victorian schools in the locality, which children can use to consider the changes that have occurred in the way schools are designed.[59] The photographs might be used to create a sequencing exercise.

Including non-local material

By drawing to an extent on imported material, the integrity of a local study need not be compromised, whilst advantage can arise because children's investigations can be extended and deepened. For instance, references are often found in Victorian school log books to object lessons, with accompanying lists of objects to be studied. The form and purposes of these lessons is not stated in the log books, but by bringing in evidence from other sources, children can appreciate what was involved in teaching object lessons. And they might be asked to design their own examples. The matter is considered further in chapter 5. It may also be the case that, as they undertake a local study, children raise unanticipated questions that cannot be addressed from the evidence that is locally available.

Progression matters and the National Curriculum

Children are expected to deepen and extend their historical competences as they proceed through their programmes of study. For each key stage, the revised National Curriculum gives brief statements relating to these matters, the difference between them indicating the nature and degree of progression that children should achieve. In the discussion that follows, examples are noted of the way in which local history provision can help to meet a selection of these requirements and hence of the role it can play in generating more challenging activities at each key stage.[60]

Key stage 1

Included amongst the requirements at this stage are developing an awareness of the past; identifying similarities and differences between ways of life at different periods; and asking and answering questions about the past. These requirements can be coupled with the view that suitable topics for this age range are family history, local history and fieldwork, study of artefacts and dramatisation of the past.[61]

The importance of family history - which can have close links with local history - in meeting these requirements is highlighted in National Curriculum documentation. For example, that of 2007 stipulates that key stage 1 children should learn about 'changes in their own lives and the way of life of their family or others around

59 A particularly useful source on the design of Victorian schools is E. E. Robson, *School Architecture* (1972 reprint of 1874 edition).

60 For consideration of progression in teaching and learning history at primary level based on the cognitive thread of Bloom's taxonomy of educational objectives, see L. Dixon and A. Hales, *Bringing History Alive through Local People and Places* (Routledge, 2014), pp.174-9. Other contributions to the theme include P. Hoodless, *Teaching History in Primary Schools* (Sage, 2008), ch.4 and A. Ford, 'Setting us free? Building meaningful models of progression for a "post-levels" world', *Teaching History*, 157 (December, 2014), pp.28-41.

61 J. Blyth, *History in Primary Schools* (Open University Press, 1989), p.7.

them'.[62] The 2014 version of the National Curriculum overlooks this aspect, however. Of course, family history matters can still be addressed and since they permit ready access to the oral, visual and artefact evidence that families possess, they have high use value in introducing young children to aspects of local history. As Alan Hodkinson suggests, children can construct their own personal timelines, illustrated by photographs or drawings, which can be extended into the lives of their parents and grandparents.[63] Amongst the benefits they can derive from so doing is an appreciation that past events in the family took place at different times. For example, grandfather's childhood occurred longer ago than father's. In other words, past family events can be placed in sequence, one of the three types of activity that, Keith Barton maintains, children need to address in developing their understanding of time.[64] Other benefits seen to arise from this type of provision are an appreciation that adults can have differing views about their past experiences and that notable changes have occurred in the types of consumer goods made available to family members from one generation to another.[65] Children's toys and clothes are cited as examples. Yet Penelope Harnett sounds a note of caution with family history studies, noting that they have the potential to be emotive and controversial and so need to be dealt with sensitively and 'with an awareness of different home situations and family structures'.[66]

When using artefacts from the past, children might observe, or preferably handle, examples that were made and/or used locally. In undertaking a school-based project on the Victorian period with year 1 and year 2 children, Pat Hoodless was able to draw on artefacts provided by the local community, as well as by the school. Part of the project involved creating two play areas for the children, one featuring domestic artefacts and the other school artefacts. Amongst the issues arising was that of how far teacher intervention should take place, given the risk that the children's own thinking and imagination might be stifled. In the event, giving some guidance on handling the artefacts was found to be necessary.[67]

---

62 The 2007 document can be viewed at <http://webarchive.nationalarchives.gov.uk/20100202100434/curriculum.qcda.gov.uk/>.

63 A. Hodkinson, 'Enhancing temporal cognition, practical activities for the primary classroom', *Primary History*, 28 (May, 2001), pp.11-12.

64 The other two are grouping historical items together, so children recognise a set of events belongs to a designated era, and measuring, which involves using dates to identify how many years ago an event occurred or the duration of past events. See K. C. Barton, 'Helping students make sense of historical time', *Primary History*, 37 (Summer, 2004), pp.13-14.

65 *National Curriculum History Working Party, Interim Report* (Department of Education and Science and the Welsh Office, 1989), pp.58-9.

66 P. Harnett, 'Foundation stage and key stage 1 history [early years]: history and citizenship education – teaching sensitive issues, part 1', *Primary History*, 45 (Spring, 2007), p.32. Further guidance on teaching family history in primary schools can be found in H. Cooper, *The Teaching of History in Primary Schools* (Fulton, third edition, 2000), pp.54-64; Dixon and Hales, *History Alive*, pp.58-79; H. Pluckrose, *Children Learning History* (Blackwell, 1991), pp.51-92; E. M. Corrigan, 'Battling on: family history in the primary classroom', *Teaching History*, 81 (October, 1995), pp.14-18; and S. Kirkland, 'Learning about the past through "ourselves and our families"', *Primary History*, 75 (Spring, 2017), pp.6-7. Also useful is D. J. Steel and L. Taylor, *Family History in Schools* (Phillimore, 1973), which includes teachers' reports of family history work carried out in both primary and secondary schools and puts forward a three-phase programme on which family history studies can be based.

67 P. Hoodless, 'A Victorian case study: simulating aspects of Victorian life in the classroom',

Key stage 2

At this stage, one requirement is that children should regularly address and sometimes devise historically valid questions about change and continuity, cause and consequence, similarity and difference and significance. The progression issue implied here is that of focusing attention on historical issues that are clearly defined and are seen to have significance in terms of promoting historical understanding. As far as local history is concerned, both dimensions are likely to be realised when linkage is made with national themes that are widely acknowledged to be of historical interest and importance, such as the impact of World War II on domestic life. But a wide range of local history studies that stand in their own right can also meet these criteria. In either case the expectation is that children will go beyond merely describing circumstances and events of the past and routinely engage with the key concepts that deepen their historical understanding. The causes and consequences of change are likely to figure strongly here. Additionally, local history studies can readily accommodate the contextualisation implied by engaging with similarity and difference. It might be, for example, that the wartime domestic life in one locality is compared with that of another or with more general findings at national level.

The point about *sometimes* devising historically valid questions implies that, for the most part, such questions will be formulated by teachers. Yet attention has been drawn to the importance of children developing this competency if they are to pursue an effective enquiry approach in their historical studies. Margaret Parsons introduces a progression dimension into the issue by urging that, from the earliest years of their education, ways should be found of helping children to pose appropriate questions. She also points to the difficulties that can arise in so doing. If the questions children devise are too broad, she observes, the investigations they undertake can become overwhelming. Yet if the questions are too narrow, insufficient information may be available to address them.[68]

One way of helping children to formulate relevant questions is to encourage them to look for further opportunities that arise from the local investigations in which they engage. John Robertson's work with primary school children in an Ayrshire village provides an example. Using1881 census schedules, the children plotted an age distribution graph for the village, dividing the population into ten-year age groups. Amongst their findings was a marked and unexpected dip in the number of young adults. This led to questions being asked about the causes, leading to further investigations and to the conclusion that, after other possibilities had been eliminated, an earlier outbreak of cholera was the likely cause.[69]

Further progression is seen to be achieved at key stage 2 through children understanding that knowledge of the past is constructed from a range of sources. One implication here is that they will become much more aware than hitherto of

---

Primary History, 7 (June, 1994), pp.14-16.

68 M. Parsons, 'Asking the right questions: a study of the ability of KS 2 children to devise and use questions as part of their own research', *Primary History*, 26 (October, 2000), pp.12-13.

69 J. W. Robertson, '"No one else knows this": Scottish primary schools using ICT to investigate local history', *Primary History*, 29 (October, 2001), pp.7-9.

value of written sources, with which they will have had little engagement at key stage 1. Equally, they may be introduced to other types of non-written source material, as well as continuing to use further examples of the types they know about. If, as is also stipulated, they are to 'construct informed responses that involve the thoughtful selection and organisation of relevant historical material', then direct engagement with these sources in investigating particular themes will be required. Thus, using several photocopied pages from one or more local school log books, children might extract details about, say, attendance, as part of an investigation into school life in the past. As one of the exercises in chapter 5 demonstrates, they might compile a report on the reasons given for scholars' absenteeism, perhaps making comparison with the present day, and consider, perhaps through teacher-led discussion, why the issue was so important to head teachers. They might also compare their findings with those they can obtain from log books relating to localities elsewhere, looking for both similarities and differences in patterns of absenteeism. Log book extracts might be used along similar lines to explore other themes relating to school life, including the nature of the curriculum, the treatment of scholars and the structure of the school day.

Key stage 3

At this stage, children are apparently required to move from devising historically valid questions to framing historically valid enquiries. The distinction could be seen in terms of children still raising appropriate questions to address during investigations they undertake, but also helping to plan at least some aspects of these investigations. They might do so from the outset of a study unit and in relation to the unit as a whole. But they might also plan elements of the study as investigation unfolds and unforeseen opportunities arise. The stipulation that they need only do so on occasions again applies, so that, for the most part, the planning function remains the responsibility of the teacher. Since there is no obligation for children to frame enquiries in every course unit they take, they need not necessarily do so when dealing with local history. Yet, given the freedom of choice that arises in selecting local history themes, units of study based on them can play a useful role in meeting this requirement, especially when linkage is made with more general historical themes. The point here is that starting from a national or international perspective should help children to identify themes they can explore at local level, along with the type of primary source material they might use and the methods they might adopt. One teaching strategy might be to encourage class discussion to identify possibilities and formulate plans. Plainly, the constraints that arise will need to be borne in mind, especially concerning resource provision and the time that can be made available for planned investigations to take place.

The other major challenge specified at this level concerns the 'rigorous use of historical sources'. Precisely what is meant by the word 'rigorous' at this level in not defined, but the implication is that, in undertaking historical investigation, children should not accept the evidence they use without making evaluations of it. Problems associated with inaccuracy, incompleteness and bias can easily present traps for the unwary, though insights into them can be difficult or impossible to obtain. It may be that recourse to other types of evidence can provide help. For instance, as discussed in chapter 9, some details of insanitary urban housing conditions described in early Victorian public health reports can sometimes be checked using evidence obtained from contemporaneous large-scale Ordnance Survey maps. Confined back yards and the provision of open cesspits within them are cases in point. And children might be asked to decide whether or not the evidence presented in these reports is likely to have described typical housing conditions or to have concentrated on the worst examples. Again, large-scale maps can shed light on the matter, since they reveal that, in some respects at least, the quality of houses provided for ordinary families varied appreciably.

Of course, in recognising the limitations of primary evidence, children should not be put off from drawing conclusions based on it. But they can be encouraged to recognise and articulate the uncertainties arising in undertaking their investigations and to realise that the interpretations they make may well need to be qualified.

Conclusion

Including local history units in the school curriculum requires several matters to be considered. Foremost amongst them is that of the theme to be addressed. Whilst a wide choice exists, resource availability will act as a greater constraint in some localities than in others, especially with regard to physical forms of evidence. There is also the question of whether local dimensions might form part of more general units of study, since local history provision need not be confined to a single theme.

Irrespective of whether or not the National Curriculum is being followed, thought will need to be given to the nature of the work in local history that children undertake at each key stage. Providing opportunities for them to acquire and demonstrate more sophisticated levels of understanding as they proceed through the key stages is a basic requirement in planning all dimensions of the history curriculum. The revised National Curriculum is far less prescriptive and detailed on this matter than previously, a development that might well be welcomed. And it may be that suitable advice is now being offered. The crucial consideration, however, is the need to move children beyond merely finding out about aspects of the locality in the past. This objective can be achieved by engaging them in focused studies that deal in some depth with themes of historical importance and that lead them to be aware of both the strengths and limitations of the interpretations they make. Adding a comparative dimension to their work can be of further help in this respect.

Conclusion

Part II
Exercises in local history

Chapter 5
School life in the late 19th and early 20th centuries

As noted in chapter 2, school log book entries can be used to facilitate investigation into several aspects of school life in the past.[70] Their use seems to have been particularly favoured at primary level, including key stage 1. Thus Jo Barkham has remarked on the many questions that her year 2 class raised when extracts from their school's log books were read to them. And more questioning arose when they were given photocopies from the log book to examine.[71]

The exercises in this chapter link with the discussion in chapter 4 on planning a local schooling unit of study. They address the curriculum and scholars' themes, drawing particularly on school log book evidence. Key points for children to understand are the prominence of the three Rs in the school curriculum, as well as the high value that schools placed on their pupils' regular attendance. The exercises can be contextualised by alerting children to how these matters were related to the so-called payments by results system. This system was introduced in 1862 under the provisions of the Revised Code and remained in force until 1897. Details are noted below. Children might discuss whether or not they think the system was a good idea and, using log book evidence, assess the impact it had on the curriculum.

Exercise 1: Latecomers and absentees

References to the poor attendance and lateness of scholars abound in school log books. Both matters brought much concern to teachers, not least because, with the introduction of the Revised Code, school grants depended partly on attendance levels and partly on the results of annual tests in reading, writing and arithmetic (the three Rs) carried out by HMIs. Girls also had to be instructed in plain needlework. Six standards or levels of attainment were devised for the examinations and no child could be examined more than once at the same standard; children had to progress to earn the grant. A deduction was made from the grant for scholars who failed to reach the standard in each subject. For children under six, the school received a grant subject to a satisfactory report from the inspector. The system was gradually revised, so that other grant-earning subjects were allowed.[72] For instance,

---

70 Background detail on the different types of school provision in the Victorian period can be found in M. Rose, 'What the Dickens? Some views of the Victorians', *Primary History*, 34 (2003), p.20; H. Claire, 'Planning for diversity in the key stage 2 history curriculum: the Victorians', *Primary History*, 28 (May, 2001), p.7; and N. Caskey, 'A project on working-class education in the Victorian period', *Primary History*, 36 (Spring, 2004), pp.24-6.

71 J. Barkham, 'Local history and literacy using written (and other) sources', *Primary History*, 64 (Summer, 2013), pp.28-9.

72 Further details of the Revised Code can be found in S. J. Curtis, *History of Education*

history and geography were amongst the 'specific' subjects introduced in 1868.[73]

Comments made in log books on the perceived reasons for absence and lateness generally find fault with parents and scholars, but extenuating circumstances might also be reported. Thus on 19th February, 1869, the headmaster at Chapel Street British School, Blackburn in Lancashire candidly admitted that the lateness of his pupils was due to the fact that he closed the door before the proper time!

Entries from the log books of several West Sussex schools in the 1890s disclose the sorts of excuses given for pupils' absenteeism. They include children working temporarily at bird scaring, beating for shooters, haymaking and harvesting; children being needed at home; the difficulty children had in reaching school when the weather was bad – the distance from home and lack of water-tight shoes receiving mention; some children being sent back home because they were wet when they arrived and others because they showed whooping cough symptoms; children being kept from school because of a local outbreak of smallpox; and boys collecting wood for bonfire night, as well as 'carrying May poles about'.[74]

That absence from school could arise because of action taken by head teachers might not have been expected and children might be asked for their views on the matter. They might also comment on the seasonal nature of absenteeism, especially in relation to work opportunities. As regards outbreaks of disease, the impact could be marked, as the following newspaper report testifies.

SCARLET FEVER AT CASTLEFORD - A serious outbreak of scarlet fever has taken place at Nostell Colliery-row, on the estate of Lord St. Oswald, and the Sanitary Authority of the district has ordered the Wragby National Schools to be closed for not less than six weeks, as two-thirds of the children attending the school come from Nostell-row.

Source: *The Leeds Mercury*, 9th May, 1892.

in Great Britain (University Tutorial Press 1961 reprint), pp.253-67. Also included in this section of the book is a fascinating description of how school inspections were conducted.

73 Details of changes made to the Revised Code can be found in M. Sturt, *The Education of the People* (Routledge & Kegan Paul,1967), pp.344-5. From 1900, schools received a block grant and were normally required to teach English, arithmetic, geography, history, singing, physical exercises, drawing (boys) and needlework (girls). Other subjects, such as science, might also be taught where practicable. To cater for the growing number of pupils who stayed on at school, a new standard VII was introduced in 1882. See P. Gordon and D. Lawton, *Curriculum Change in the Nineteenth and Twentieth Centuries* (Hodder & Stoughton,1978), pp.5 &19. Useful detail on the Revised Code and changes made to it can also be found on the *Education in England: a history of our schools* website at <http://www.educationengland.org.uk/history/chapter03.html>.

74 The extracts form part of the *Learning Resources* section of West Sussex County Council's website, which can be viewed at <http://www.westsussex.gov.uk/learning/learning_resources.aspx>. Select the Victorian West Sussex link to reach the source gallery relating to schooling.

Coping with lateness and absenteeism

The extracts shown below are taken from the log books of three east Lancashire schools. They show how attempts were made to deal with lateness and absenteeism. Children could be given a selection of similar entries taken from school log books in their own localities, perhaps transcribed, or be challenged to make and record their own selections from photocopied pages of log books.

Dealing with absentees

This afternoon, a Merit Holiday (for attendance) was given. This is the third successive Merit Holiday (which is given for an attendance of 94% for a month ...).
(Newchurch Mixed School, Rossendale, November, 1914)

Poor attendance – sent a boy after absentees.
(Edgeside School, Rossendale, August, 1896)

Dealing with lateness

The children very late in appearing this morning. Spoke about this, and made especial reference to it, in our morning devotions.
(Chapel Street School, Blackburn, 3rd August, 1869)

I was much annoyed this morning with the latecoming. Kept a number of boys in to make up their lost lessons.
(Chapel Street School, Blackburn, 25th August, 1869)

Classroom activities

Children could consider how successful the various policies adopted to deal with latecomers and absentees were likely to have been. The extracts give them some help, but they will need to think around the issues, perhaps drawing on their own experiences. The work could be undertaken in two stages. Firstly, they could write down arguments for and against each policy. Secondly, using these arguments, they could grade each policy according to the likely degree of success. Arguments arising during the first part of the exercise, which might result from group discussion, could be recorded in the type of worksheet shown below.

Children could decide that awarding merit holidays (providing an incentive) and keeping in (giving a punishment) would have been more effective in encouraging attendance than sending boys after absentees and speaking about lateness. Indeed, as the extracts show, the Chapel Street school head teacher had to take sterner measures than merely speaking about the matter. Class discussion could emphasise the difficulty of reaching clear-cut conclusions with this type of analysis and of coping satisfactorily with lateness and absenteeism. These points could be reinforced by considering other means that could be employed to cope with the problems, such as giving individual prizes for good attendance.

Dealing with latecomers and absentees

1. To help you decide how well these policies might have worked, think of arguments for and against each one. Discuss them and then write them down in the table below.

Policy	Arguments for	Arguments against
Merit holiday	*Evidence in extract shows it had been successful for three months.*	*Would not work when disease outbreaks occurred, causing many pupils to be absent.*
	Gives children an incentive to attend.	*Quite a high attendance was required – hard to achieve.*
Sending boy after absentees	*He might know where to find his fellow pupils.*	*He might find them but be unable to bring them back.*
Spoke about coming late	*Some pupils might respond.*	*No strong threats or incentives given.*
		Absentees would not hear the appeal.
Keeping children in	*Children had to make up the lost time.*	*Parents might object to their children being kept in.*
	They still had to do the lessons they missed.	*The teachers would have extra work to do.*

2. Decide whether each policy was likely to have been

   (a) very successful (b) quite successful (c) not very successful.

3. Which do you think would have been the most successful policy? Say why.

   ....

   ....

   ....

Question 3 on the worksheet is included in order to encourage children to reach an overall conclusion on the basis of the evidence presented. The intention is that they will make a reasoned judgement, showing an appreciation of the difficulties involved.

Matters arising

There is scope for children to contextualise their findings by making comparisons with log book evidence on absenteeism from other localities, including West Sussex. They might also consider how far the reasons for children's absenteeism in the past, and the policies adopted to counteract it, still apply. Initiatives such as breakfast clubs might be noted.

The point might also be brought out that absence was seen as a problem by the head teacher, but not necessarily by the children or their parents. From their perspectives, the opportunity to earn money from temporary work and therefore contribute to family income, or to take on domestic duties when needed to meet some sort of family crisis, could be seen to have outweighed any advantage that arose from going to school for a while.

Exercise 2: School timetables

To engage more deeply with the question of the importance the three Rs assumed in those schools that derived income from annual inspections, school timetables need to be considered. Examples relating to particular localities may not be easy to find, so reliance may have to be made on timetables from elsewhere. Two examples are given below. The first was used at Edgeside Infants' School, in Rossendale, Lancashire during May, 1875. The second, dating from 1895, was used at Standard I level in the boys' section of the British School at Hitchin, Hertfordshire.[75] The timetables vary in format, but both reveal the predominance of the three Rs. There was some similarity in the other subjects taught, with object lessons, singing and art work (drawing at Hitchen and form and colour at Edgeside) being mentioned.

Scrutiny of these timetables enables several matters about school life to be addressed.

Daily Time Table

9.00 to 9.20	*Examination of Home Work: Register Marked and Closed before 9.20.*
9.20 to 9.50	*Writing.*
9.50 to 10.20	*Reading.*
10.20 to 10.50	*Arithmetic.*
10.50 to 11.00	*Recreation: Singing or Drill in Wet Weather.*
11.00 to 11.30	*Writing Figures.*
11.30 to 12.00	*Form and Colour Mon., Wed., Fri.,: Object Lessons Tue. & Thu.*
2.00 to 2.15	*Registers Marked and Closed before 2.15.*
2.15 to 3.00	*Writing.*
3.00 to 3.15	*Arithmetic.*
3.15 to 3.25	*Recreation: Singing or Drill in Wet Weather.*
3.25 to 3.55	*Reading.*
3.55 to 4.30	*Singing Mon., Wed., & Fri.: Tables Tue. & Thu.*

Edgeside timetable

75 The boys' school timetable is reproduced in F. Dodwell, 'The Jill Grey collection and Hitchin British schools', *Primary History*, 27 (January 2001), pp.19-24.

Time	Monday	Tuesday	Wednesday	Thursday	Friday
9.10 - 9.50	Reading	Reading	Reading	Writing	Scripture
10.00 - 10.55	Writing	Transcription	Writing	Drawing	Drawing
11.10 - 12.00	Arithmetic	Arithmetic	Arithmetic	Arithmetic	Arithmetic
2.15 - 2.50	Writing	Reading	Arithmetic	Arithmetic	Copy Books
2.50 - 3.25	Reading	Drawing	Repetition	Reading	Object Lesson
3.25 - 4.20	Geography	Arithmetic	Spelling	Geography	Singing

Hitchin timetable

Classroom activities

Children will need an introduction to the source and some discussion of its content. They might then tackle a worksheet containing questions about the organisation of the school day and the range and relative importance of the subjects taught. Questions might include:

1. Which were the three most important subjects taught?
2. What other subjects were taught?
3. How long did the children have for playtime in the morning and afternoon?
4. How long was the dinner-time break?
5. How long is your dinner-time break?
6. Why do you think the Victorian scholars had a much longer dinner-time break than you have? (Clue: the Victorian school would not have had a kitchen.)
7. At what times did the school day start and end?
8. At what times does your school day start and end?
9. How long was the school day then?
10. How long is your school day?
11. Say whether you prefer having your own school timetable or a timetable from a Victorian school. Give reasons for your answer.

Matters arising

One point that emerges clearly is the lengthy break that occurred at dinner time, the children generally going home to eat. Perhaps around two hours was a common length of time for a dinner break. Variations doubtless occurred, but the crucial point is that children needed a longer dinner break than would have been the case had they all been able to eat at school.

One reason for extending the dinner-time break is found in an entry made in the log book of Newchurch School, Rossendale, in September, 1894. It reads:

> In order to allow children to take dinners to the mills, the whole of them are now dismissed at 11.55.

By how much the break was extended is not stated.

There is obvious scope for children to compare the Victorian scholars' timetables with their own, looking for elements of continuity as well as of change. The impact of providing school dinners on site, along with the continuing importance attached to the three Rs, are cases in point. In so doing, they will give context to their findings. They might also consider the reasons for both the changes and the continuities that they note. If local timetables from the Victorian period are available, comparisons might also be made with those from Hitchin and Edgeside.

Exercise 3: Object lessons

School log books frequently give lists of object lessons, which formed part of the curriculum that children experienced during and beyond the Victorian period. The lists can include a wide range of items such as animals, plants, food, clothes and household goods. Since object lessons will be unfamiliar to present-day children, and quite possibly to their teachers, some explanation is needed about the form they took and the purposes they had.

Of help in these respects is the *Manual for Infant Teachers*, the fifth edition of which was published by the Home and Colonial School Society in 1884.[76] This book gives several examples of object lessons, detailing how they should be taught to infants and the purpose of so doing. Thus the objects given in one of the lists provided in the book were chosen 'to lead to observation of parts', whilst those in an accompanying list sought 'to develop some striking characteristic or quality'.[77]

To illustrate the approach that teachers might have adopted, object lessons dealing with a pencil and with paper may be considered. They are set out below. The former aimed to highlight uses as well as parts and the latter, not without health and safety concerns, 'to develop the idea of inflammable'. Both were to be covered within a single lesson and the teacher was exhorted to make much use of the big slate, so that when 'each part or quality of the object is brought out, the first letter of the word expressing it should be printed on the slate'.[78]

Object lesson on a pencil

Who can tell the use of a pencil? - *It is used for writing.*

Do any of you know any other uses of a pencil? Some child will perhaps say – *It is used to draw with.*

Repeat together – *"A pencil is used to write with, and to draw with."*

If you wished to write or draw, could you do if you had a pencil alone, and nothing more? – *No. You must have paper, or something to write or draw upon.*

Now look well at the pencil, and tell me if it is everywhere alike, as this piece of chalk is. What can any of you see? – *The wood of the pencil.*

76 The society was established in 1836 to train teachers and improve infant education. Brief details are given at <http://www.ucl.ac.uk/bloomsbury-project/institutions/home_and_colonial.htm>.

77 *Infant School Manual*, Pt 2, pp.79-82.

78 *Infant School Manual*, Pt 2, p.80.

What more? – *The lead of it.*

The wood is not then the whole of the pencil? *What is it? It is a part of it.*

And what is the lead? *The lead is also part of the pencil.*

What can you say the pencil has? *The pencil has parts.*

Try and find some other parts. Call a child to touch some part of the pencil. He will most likely touch the ends; the children may not know how to call them; they may be told they are the ends of the pencil, and then repeat together – "*The pencil has ends*".

Look at the ends, and tell me what you see? *The lead.*

Yes; the lead runs all through the pencil. Before anyone can use the pencil for writing, what must be done to one of the ends? *It must be cut.*

What do we form when we cut it? *We form a point.*

What more do you see on the pencil? *Some words.*

That is the maker's name. Now repeat together the parts a pencil has – *'A pencil has wood,' &c.*

What would be the consequence do you think if the pencil were all lead? The lead would easily break, and it would blacken our fingers.

Now tell us where the lead is? Repeat together – "*The lead runs along the middle of the pencil.*"

Where is the wood? Repeat together – "*The wood is round the lead.*"

Where is the point? Repeat together – "*The point is at one end of the pencil.*"

Object lesson on paper

What is this? *It is a piece of paper.*

Repeat together – "*This is paper.*"

Which of you can tell me any use which is made of paper? Yes: it is used for writing upon. Have you seen it used for any other purpose? Is it used for lighting fires? *Yes.*

Can you tell me any other things used for fires? *Coal and wood.*

Let us see if we can find out why paper is used. How does mother light the fire when she has put the things in the grate? *She uses a match.*

Here is a match. I will strike it. What do you see now on the match? *Some fire.*

Yes. Fire like this is called a flame. Now I will put the paper in the flame. What do you see on the paper? *More flame.*

What will become of the paper if we let it go on burning? *It will all burn away.*

Now perhaps you can tell me why paper is used in a fire. "*Yes, teacher: because it will burn.*"

Tell me what we see when it is burning? *A flame.*

Now repeat – "*Paper will burn with a flame.*"

Name other things which will burn with a flame.

Classroom activities

Following explanation of the nature and purpose of object lessons, children might take part in a short, teacher-prepared object lesson, perhaps drawing on the examples shown above and perhaps avoiding some of the questions that might lead to unwelcome responses! They might be given sheets containing some of the expected responses, which they could read out together. Other responses would not be given, but, once correctly determined, could be repeated by all the class.

Working in groups, children might then try to devise short object lessons of their own, providing both questions and responses. The challenge in doing so might relate to either the parts and uses of objects or their properties. They might choose an object from one of the lists in a log book from their own locality.

Matters arising

Judging from the examples, the teaching approach was to elicit as much response from the scholars as possible using a carefully-structured set of questions and to reinforce their understanding by getting them to repeat out loud the desired answers. However, as with the ends of the pencil, it was permissible to tell the children the required answer when uncertainty arose or was anticipated. Plainly, some responses required of the children were more demanding than others.

Object lessons could be made more challenging by incorporating a comparative dimension. For instance, the *Manual for Infant Teachers* contains an object lesson that asks children to compare a quill pen with a lead pencil, focusing on the qualities of each.[79]

A plethora of object lessons and how they might be conducted can be found in A. S. Welch, *Object Lessons: Prepared for Teachers of Primary Schools and Primary Classes* (1862). Welch held the view that 'the first instruction given to a child in school should be based on the fact that his intellectual activity consists in hearing and seeing rather than in reasoning and reflecting'. He believed that encouraging children between the ages of 5 and 10 to engage in abstract thinking should be avoided.[80]

79 *Infant School Manual*, Pt 3, pp.137-8.

80 The book can be viewed on-line at <https://archive.org/details/objectlessonspreoowelcrich>.

Chapter 6

Naming local children in Tudor times

For the exercise discussed in this chapter, children use evidence from local parish baptism registers to determine which forenames were the most popular in late Elizabethan times, what type of considerations influenced forename selection during this period and, through comparison with the present day, how and why forename popularity has changed over time. Additionally, in developing their understanding of these matters, they can engage with numeracy and ICT applications, particularly through compiling forename percentages and frequency distributions.[81]

To illustrate the approach, the exercise draws on baptisms recorded at Barnstaple in Devon between 1590 and 1593. These have been transcribed and published and can be viewed online at
<https://archive.org/stream/registerofbaptisoobyubarn#page/n7/mode/2up>.

Earlier years within the Tudor period could have been selected for the exercise, but forename information from West Yorkshire is available for the early 1590s, which can be used for comparative purposes. It is given later in the chapter.

As noted in chapter 2, many transcriptions of parish registers have been published and they are increasingly being made available online, especially as part of the *Online Parish Clerks*' project. Accordingly, the exercise can easily be replicated in other localities, as well as being set in later time periods. To give context, it could form part of the *People on the Move* local study unit mentioned in chapter 4, since, through the ages, migration helps to explain the emergence over time of a growing variety in children's forenames. The exercise also links with the National Curriculum aim of children knowing and understanding how Britain has been influenced by the wider world.

Extracting the evidence

Children could work in pairs or small groups, either from online parish register transcripts or from photocopies of printed registers held in local libraries. Decisions are needed about the total number of baptisms that will be extracted and about how many entries each pair or group should extract. With regard to the former, even quite small numbers – say 50 or so – are likely to reveal that some forenames of both boys and girls were much more popular than others. But samples that total at least 100 male and 100 female names will give more certain

81 The linkage with numeracy in this exercise and the exercises in other chapters is intended to demonstrate how children can deploy basic mathematical techniques in helping them to interpret and present historical findings. For discussion on the matter, and further examples, see I. Phillips, 'History and mathematics or history with mathematics: does it add up?', *Teaching History*, 107 (June, 2002), pp.35-40.

results. If each pair or small group of children in a class extracted and recorded about 20 entries, enough evidence would certainly be generated.

Using a computer spreadsheet, the children could construct a grid, creating a list of the frequency with which forenames occur in each month. An example recording the boys' names given in the Barnstaple register during 1790 is shown below. The advantage of working in this way is that checks can easily be made on the accuracy of the recording as each month is completed. Additionally, the spreadsheet will add the total number of names recorded. The importance of extracting information accurately and of making checks should be stressed. That two columns are needed to record March entries is because, until 1752, the new year in Britain began on 25th March (Lady Day). The girls' names for 1790 could continue the list or a separate list could be compiled. Spreadsheets can become too big to use easily, however, so it may be best to create a new one for each year that is selected. Alternatively, children could record their findings by hand. They will need sheets of lined paper on which grids with 15 columns can be created.

Barnstaple baptisms, 1790

Name	Mar	Apr	May	Jun	Jul	Aug	Sep	Oct	Nov	Dec	Jan	Feb	Mar	Total
John	1	11		1	1	11	11		111	11	11	1	111	20
Richarde	1							1					1	3
Nycholas		11								1				3
Lewis		1												1
Thomas		1								1				2
Phillip		1												1
Willyam			1		1			1						3
Eusebeus			1											1
Samuell				1										1
George				1					1	111			1	6
Roberte					1		1							2
Arthur					1									1
James						11	1							3
Peter							1		1					2
Water							1							1
Anthonie							1							1
Trystram											1			1
Henrye												1		1
Stevin													1	1
														54

In creating the spreadsheet, the columns can be narrowed as the recording for each month is completed. In this way, the column in which the results are being recorded becomes wider than the preceding columns, making it easier to identify.

One other point should be made. The name spellings used by those entering the baptisms often differ from place to place and from present-day forms. They can also differ within a particular register, perhaps because different people made the entries. For the most part, children will be able to cope with the variations, but they may need some help, not least to ensure that the names they record are standardised.

Presenting the results

Children might display the results of their counts in tabular form in order to show frequency distributions for girls' names and boys' names. The example given below uses the results from the Barnstaple register counts for 1590-93. Since the point of the exercise is to identify the most popular names that were recorded in the register, names that appear fewer than three times during these years have been excluded. The name spellings that, for the most part, appear in the register have been kept.

Girls' names	Number	Boys' names	Number
Marye	35	John	46
Elizabeth	18	Willyam	13
Angnis	11	George	11
Johan	11	Richard	10
Catherin	9	Nycholas	9
Margaret	7	Thomas	9
Prycilla	7	James	7
Grace	6	Roberte	6
Anne	4	Walter	4
Honor	4	Arthur	3
Latis	4	Roger	3
Thamsin	4		
Alse	3		
Dorothie	3		

The results of the searches can also be displayed as a bar chart. That relating to the Barnstable girls' names is shown below.

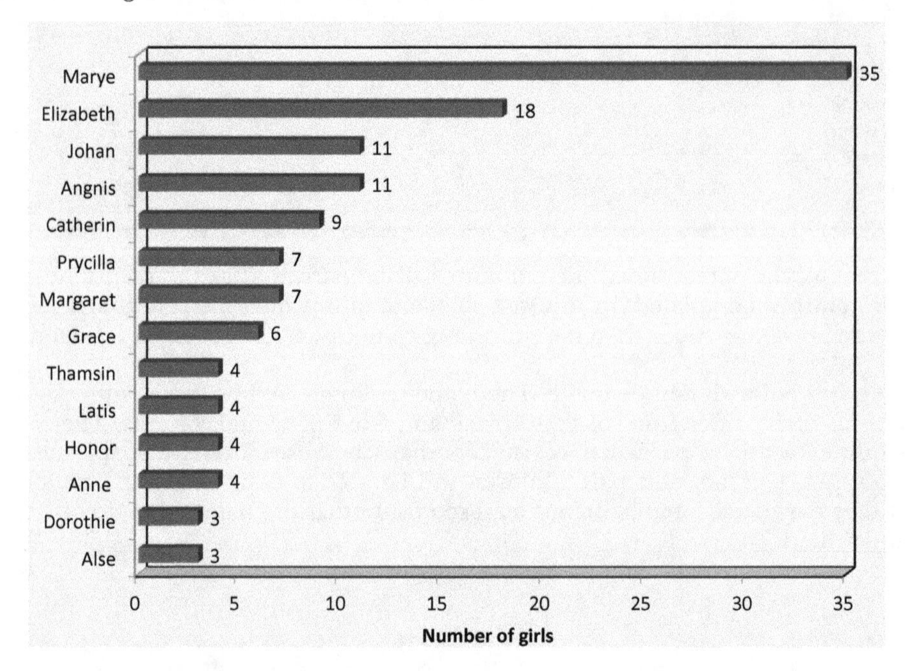

Interpreting the findings

A key conclusion children will draw from their investigations is that, for both boys and girls, a few names were far more popular than others. Thus the predominance of John and Mary is particularly striking in the case of the Barnstaple sample. Discussion might take place with the children on why some forenames became so popular. Revered biblical figures are one possibility. John is amongst them, both as one of Jesus Christ's twelve apostles and as John the Baptist, the preacher who baptised him. And the name Johan (Joan) probably achieved popularity as the feminine form of John. Amongst them, too, is Mary, the mother of Christ and her mother Anne, Christ's grandmother. The popularity of Thomas as a name may also link with the bible, through Thomas the Apostle, another of Christ's twelve apostles, but also with the martyred Thomas Becket, the Archbishop of Canterbury, who was canonised soon after his death in 1170. The names of other popular saints were also likely to have been influential in naming children. They include St. George, the patron saint of England who was famous for his chivalry, and St. Agnes, the young teenager from Rome who was famed for her devotion to Christianity and who was martyred in 307 AD. It should also be appreciated that, following the conquest of 1066, Norman names became increasingly fashionable and those of popular monarchs in the post-conquest era may have provided inspiration for many parents in naming their children. William I, who carried out the 1066 invasion, and Richard I ('Lionheart') the warrior king who led the Third Crusade, are examples. The achievements of Elizabeth I may also have encouraged parents to name their children after her, but they may also have looked to another biblical person, namely Elizabeth, mother of John the Baptist.[82]

The Barnstaple names in context

Further analysis arises if children calculate the proportions that the most common names comprise in the samples they take. Those for the Barnstaple sample are given below.

Girls' names	Percentage	Boys' names	Percentage
Most common (Mary)	22	Most common (John)	29
Two most common (Mary & Elizabeth)	33	Two most common (John & William)	37
Three most common (Mary, Elizabeth & Agnes/Joan)	48	Three most common (John, William & George)	50

As can be seen the three most popular names for boys reached half the total, whilst the two most popular formed over a third and the most popular exceeded a quarter.

82 For further discussion on the origins of forenames, see P. Hanks, K. Hardcastle and F. Hodges, *A Dictionary of First Names* (Oxford University Press, second edition, 2006). Local libraries often have a copy.

The distribution was similar for girls' names, with slightly lower percentage returns in each category.

Context 1: comparison with other parishes

How typical were such proportions in the early 1590s? To shed some light on this matter, children can compare the findings from the samples they take with those from Barnstaple. There are also published examples that can help, including that shown below, which is derived from 300 baptisms recorded at Leeds between 1590 and 1593.[83]

Girls' names	Percentage	Boys' names	Percentage
Most common (Elizabeth)	14	Most common (William)	18
Two most common (Elizabeth & Anne)	27	Two most common (William & Thomas)	33
Three most common (Elizabeth, Anne & Alice)	38	Three most common (William, Thomas & John)	45

The Leeds figures again show marked concentrations in children's names, though, as might be expected at local level, they differ from those at Barnstaple. Somewhat lower concentrations are evident and only Elizabeth, John and William are amongst the three most popular names in each sample.

Some idea of national trends in forename popularity can be obtained from a sample of 122,710 names drawn from baptism registers in 40 English parishes. They provide rankings of forename popularity by decade between 1538 and 1700. Key findings are:

- Throughout this period, John occupied first position amongst boys' names, whilst William and Thomas shared second and third places and Richard and Robert shared fourth and fifth places.
- Amongst girls' names, Joan headed the list in the 1540s, but fell steadily during the period, occupying tenth position in the 1690s.
- Elizabeth was in first or second position throughout the period, whilst Mary gained ground, becoming first or second during the 17th century.
- Anne also gained ground, rising from seventh in the 1550s to occupy third position throughout the 17th century.
- Jane became a more popular name, too, rising from eighth or ninth position in the 16th century to become normally fifth or sixth in the 17th century.[84]

83 Figures are also given for Halifax. See G. Redmonds, *Christian Names in Local and Family History* (Dundurn, 2004), pp.140-5.

84 S. Smith-Bannister, *Names and Naming Patterns in England, 1538-1750* (Oxford University Press, 1997), Pt.3 and Appendix C. The figures are reproduced in Redmonds, *Christian Names,* Appendix 2.

- Mary, John and William remained amongst the most popular three names into the early decades of the 20th century, though they occupied decreasing proportions of the total range of names children were given.[85]

Context 2: comparison with present-day names

In order to consider change over time, children might compare present-day name popularity with that in times past. The *Behind the Name* website, which, for England and Wales, draws on data from the Office for National Statistics, will be of especial help to them. It can be viewed at <http://www.behindthename.com/top/>.

The table below records the most popular names given to babies in England and Wales in 2012. When compared with the tables showing 16th century names, two major differences are apparent. One is that the most common names for both boys and girls have come to comprise insignificant proportions – just 1.9 and 2.0 per cent respectively. The other is that the most common names have changed, though Jack can be seen as the diminutive form of John. Also, several of the boys' names remain amongst the most popular. Thus Thomas and William rank sixth and ninth respectively and are closely followed by James in 10th position and George in 12th. On the other hand, Richard is 249th in the list. As far as girls' names are concerned, the move away from the more popular names of past centuries is more marked. Thus Elizabeth is in 37th position, whilst Anna (a variant of Anne) is 68th and Mary is as far down as 241st.

Girls' names	Percentage	Boys' names	Percentage
Most common (Amelia)	2.0	Most common (Harry)	1.9
Two most common (Amelia & Olivia)	3.3	Two most common (Harry & Oliver)	3.7
Three most common (Amelia, Olivia & Jessica)	4.5	Three most common (Harry, Oliver & Jack)	5.4

Matters arising

Children might be asked for their explanations of why a far greater range of forenames is now available than in the past. They might reflect on the growing contacts made with overseas countries as British people increasingly visit them and as more overseas visitors come to Britain; immigrants bringing new names into the country; and the rise of a global media, which draws attention to a rich variety of forenames, including those of favourite celebrities in various walks of life. These influences have been exerted much more strongly during the post-World War II years than previously, giving children the opportunity to engage with the idea of the varying pace at which change over time can occur.

85 Details can be found in D. A. Galbi, *Long-Term Trends in Personal Given Name Frequencies in the UK* (2002), which can be viewed on line at <http://www.galbithink.org/names.htm>.

Additional talking points about naming practices concern children being given the same forename as their parents. Children might find examples in the baptism register sheets they use, though, especially during the 16th century, baptism register entries might omit both parents' forenames or give only that of the father. Where both parents are named, a gender dimension can be introduced into the analysis, so that children can see if the practice was more common with boys' names than with girls' names. The findings arising might be linked with the notion of 'family' names being passed down the generations. There is also the matter of children being given more than one forename, a practice that has become more fashionable over time, giving people more distinctive identities, even when a family name is iincluded

Chapter 7

Road travellers in early Victorian times

This chapter considers how visual evidence can be used in teaching local history. It features a poster dating from 1845 that advertises a new stagecoach service from Colne, in the uplands of north-east Lancashire, to Blackpool, then an emerging resort on the Lancashire coast. The way in which children can question visual evidence is addressed, as is the way in which evidence from written sources can be adduced to help in providing possible answers. The final section of the chapter considers other ways in which children can use visual sources in studying local history, especially through comparative analysis.

Using the poster as a source of evidence

The poster advertising the coach service is shown overleaf. The route the coach took is noted in the poster and can be seen on the accompanying map extracts. The journey length was about 48 miles and turnpike (toll) roads, much improved by gradient easing, were available between Colne and Preston. The railway lines that came to join the two towns are also shown on the map, the last link being made in May, 1846, when a branch line to Blackpool was opened from the Preston and Wyre railway near Poulton-le-Fylde (Poulton in the Fylde on the map). Thus the coach service probably had a very limited life span.

Children might begin by describing what the illustration shows, noting, for example, that a team of four horses was used to propel the coach; that some passengers travelled inside the coach and others outside; that the coach had prominent designs painted or transferred on its side panels; and that the driver used both reins and a whip to control the horses. They might then move on to make inferences, recognising the uncertainty that arises in so doing.

Questions they could be asked in making inferences include the following:

1. Do you think it would have been more comfortable to ride inside or outside the coach? Say why.
2. How do you think the outside passengers and the coachman would have reached their seats and got down from them?
3. Do you think that the inside passengers would have paid higher fares than those outside? Say why.
4. There seems to be a passenger on the roof of the stagecoach. Do you think he or she would really have ridden on the top of the coach? Give a reason for your answer.
5. The other passengers are seated two abreast. How many of them would there probably have been when the coach was full?
6. How might passengers have ensured a seat was available for them before they travelled?
7. Where might passengers' luggage have been carried on the coach?

Sea Bathing.

The Public are respectfully informed that an OMNIBUS called

THE SAFETY

Will commence Running to the SIMPSON'S HOTEL,

BLACKPOOL,

On Wednesday, the 21st May, 1845,

From the HOLE IN THE WALL INN, in COLNE,

And from the OLD RED LION INN, BURNLEY,

Through Blackburn, Preston, and Lytham to Blackpool Three Times a Week, viz.—

On Wednesdays and Fridays from Colne, starting at Six o'clock in the Morning, and leaving Burnley at Seven o'clock, and reaching Blackpool at Two o'clock in the Afternoon, and on Monday Mornings from Burnley at Seven o'clock.

The above Omnibus will leave Blackpool returning to the above places every Tuesday, Thursday, and Saturday, at Ten o'clock in the Forenoon.

N. B. Arrangements will be made so that Passengers will be able to proceed through to Blackpool, without stopping except for change of Horses.

PERFORMED BY THE PUBLIC'S MOST OBEDIENT SERVANTS,

STUTTARD, ALLEN, & Co.

Source: Pilgrim & Badgery of Colne (solicitors) archive, DDBD/57/5/2. Reproduced with permission from Lancashire Archives.

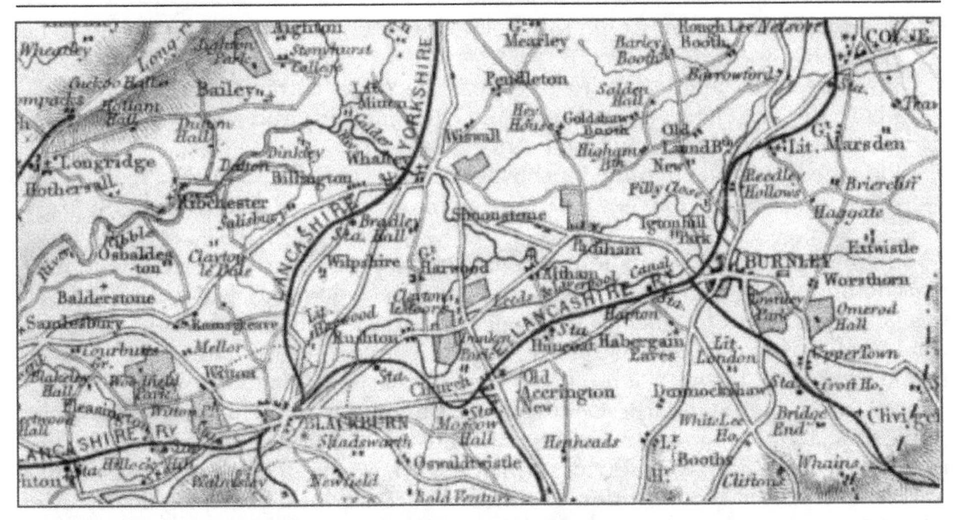

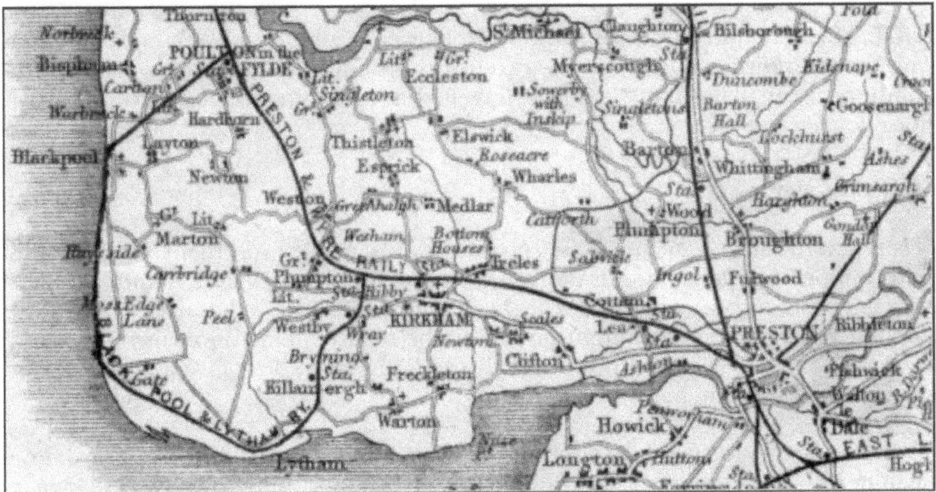

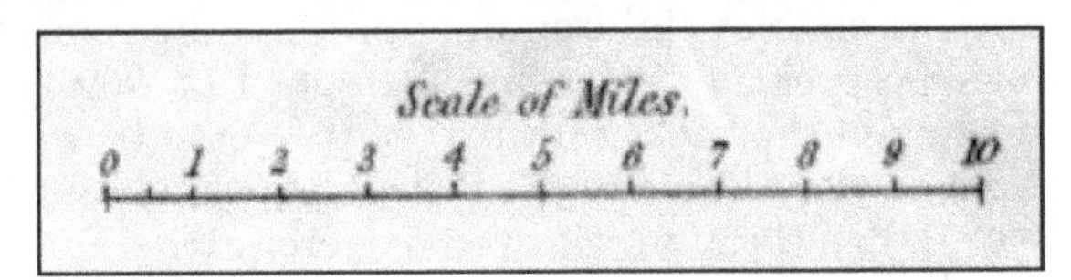

Source: Post Office map of Lancashire, North Division, 1864.

Children might also consider the symbolism of the designs on the side of the coach. The uppermost appear to be a form of the Prince of Wales feathers – a display of three white ostrich feathers – the personal badge of the heir to the British throne. Below are eight-pointed star designs, examples of which the children can make from juxtaposing two squares of paper. Such designs are seen to represent baptism, therefore providing appropriate symbols for a newly-formed stagecoach service. Whether these symbols appeared on the actual coach is unknown.

The written part of the poster provides opportunity for children to learn more about the nature of stagecoach travel. Possibilities include finding evidence to show:

- that the journey from Colne to Blackpool was not non-stop (horses had to be changed);
- why passengers might want to go to Blackpool (sea bathing);
- where the passengers started from in Colne (an inn) and where they finished their journey in Blackpool (an hotel);
- the scheduled time that the journey from Colne to Blackpool took, making the point that a return journey on the same day was not possible (8 hours).

Attention might also be given to the nature of the poster as an advertisement. One consideration here is the name given to the coach or omnibus. Calling it *The Safety* was no doubt meant to reassure passengers that they could be confident no injury would befall them. Additionally, symbolically connecting the coach service with royalty may have been an attempt to suggest that the quality of service offered aspired to very high standards. Children might also be asked to find examples of the polite tone adopted in the advertisement. Thus the public were being 'respectfully informed' about the new service, which was performed by the public's 'most obedient servant'. Opportunities for children to create local examples clearly arise.

Linking the scheduled time for the journey between Colne and Blackpool (8 hours) with the road distance between the two towns (48 miles) provides opportunity for children to calculate that the coach travelled at an average speed of 6 miles per hour.

Matters arising

Given that the stagecoach exercise is based around an advertisement, children will have opportunity to consider the reliability of historical evidence and, perhaps drawing on their own experience of travelling, to appreciate that what is stated or implied in advertisements might not always be realised. Stated journey times and seat availability are cases in point. Yet the advertisement does give a good idea of stagecoach travel times and procedures.

To provide context, the type of exercise considered here could fit into a theme dealing with the coming of the railway age in Britain. Comparing local evidence on road and rail transport enables children to appreciate the remarkable degree of change that occurred, especially regarding the speed of travel. An exercise that develops this theme and that links with part of the route between Colne and Blackpool can be found on the website of the British Association for Local History at <http://www.balh.org.uk/education/classroom-exercises>.

Bringing in further evidence

Evidence from other localities and types of source can help in addressing the questions arising from studying the poster. As far as the experience of stage coach travel is concerned, this evidence is especially instructive about the discomforts and dangers that could arise.

To begin with, an extract from a letter written in 1850 by Evan Smith, a partner in a Sheffield firm that manufactured silver-plated goods, can be quoted. He acted as the firm's sales representative and carried his samples (or patterns) with him, including such bulky items as candlesticks, tea and coffee pots and trays. These had to be packed in wooden boxes, which needed careful handling to prevent the goods being damaged in transit.[86]

> One had to go, pattens and all, outside a coach piled so high with luggage there was barely room to place your bottom, for 12 to 16 hours in cold, rain or snow and generally night through.

Evidently, some luggage was carried on top of the coach, but at the expense of passenger comfort, which could anyway be impaired by inclement weather.

Two extracts from *Tom Brown's Schooldays*, a novel written by Thomas Hughes and published in 1857, provide further insights. The book contains an account of the seventy-mile journey that Tom undertook when he left London to attend school at Rugby. His journey on the Tally-ho coach started at 3 o'clock on a cold November night.

> It was another affair altogether, a dark ride on top of the Tally-ho, I can tell you, in a tight Petersham coat and your feet dangling six inches from the floor. Then you knew what cold was, and what it was to be without legs, for not a bit of feeling you had in them after the first half hour.

When the coach stopped, Tom was told to jump down. But this was more easily said than done.

> Tom finds a difficulty in jumping, or indeed finding the top of the wheel with his feet, which may be in the next world for all he feels: so the guard picks him off the coach top and sets him on his legs ...

The first extract adds to Evan Smith's point about the discomforts that could arise from travelling on the outside of a stagecoach. The second makes it clear that disembarking from the outside seats might not be achieved without difficulty or risk!

Whether *The Safety* lived up to its name is unknown. So, too, is the general safety of stagecoach services. However, contemporary travellers have left some graphic accounts of accidents that occurred, including that involving Sir George Head.[87] During the summer of 1835, Head took the *Lake Tourist* stagecoach, which provided a daily service from Whitehaven to Workington on the Cumberland coast and then proceeded inland to Cockermouth, Keswick, Ambleside (at the north end of Lake Windermere) and on to its destination at Kendal. On boarding at Workington, he noted that the stagecoach left much to be desired, describing it as being 'ill found' and 'crazy-looking, unsteady and badly appointed altogether'. But the situation was made worse following a stop at Keswick. Additional passengers and luggage were taken on board for the onward journey to Windermere, where a regatta was being held, and Kendal. As a result, Head observed, 'the figure of the Lake Tourist

---

86 A typescript of the letter is preserved at Sheffield City Archives amongst the records left by W. & G. Sissons.

87 Sir George Head, *A Home Tour Through the Manufacturing Districts of England* during the *Summer of 1835* (Cass 1968 reprint of the 1836 edition), pp.377-88. The book can be viewed online at <http://catalog.hathitrust.org/Record/001315340>.

was completely hidden by packages that overhung the sides ...'. But, even more alarmingly, a fellow passenger had spotted a serious defect in one of the wheels – Head did not give details - and also that one of the linch pins, which held the wheels in place on their axles, was missing. All that could be found to replace the pin was a rusty nail.

Head took an outside seat. The first problem arose when the coach reached the bottom of a hill on the stretch between Keswick and Ambleside. Much to their annoyance, the passengers had to disembark and walk so the coach would become light enough for the horses to pull it up the hill. The passengers boarded the coach again at the top of the hill and the journey continued. They were within six miles of Ambleside when, Head relates, 'came the time of reckoning'.

> Proceeding at a gentle pace down a long steep hill, with a dragged off hind wheel, the coach, having overpowered the horses for a few seconds, began to rock, laying an awful stress on the springs, first lounging on one side, and then on the other, till the defective hind wheel (the near one), being the weakest point, gave way all at once, every spoke breaking close to the nave, and over went the Lake Tourist, striking the near edge of the top of the carriage within about four feet of the bottom of a seven-foot stone wall. The crash, the scream of the women, and the scramble of people among the tumbling packages, were all simultaneous; for my part I was thrown, and partly helped myself, on top of the aforesaid stone wall, where I might have sat comfortably enough on a thick bed of moss, had not many individuals required assistance.

Fortunately, the accident was less disastrous than it might have been. Several passengers lay under the coach, which 'rested most perilously above them' and they might have been crushed had not the coachman managed to keep hold of the reins and steady the horses. The worst injury amongst the passengers was a dislocated ankle. In the aftermath of the accident, disagreement ensued as to how best to proceed. One possibility was that the injured man and stagecoach driver should stay behind to guard the packages whilst the others walked to Ambleside to get help. Another was that carriages might be hired from local farmers. However, it was finally agreed that the coachman would ride one of the horses bareback to Ambleside to get help.

Matters arising

Examples of the comments that contemporary travellers made about road conditions are noted in chapter 2. The comments cited here add to the evidence they provide about the discomfort and dangers they experienced. Head's account of the accident with which he is involved is both detailed and interesting and might well be read out to children. They could be asked after hearing the account to re-create the type of discussion that took place amongst those involved in the accident as to the best way forward and the advantages and drawbacks of each proposal. A worksheet of the type shown below could be devised for the purpose. Blame for the accident might be seen to lie with the stagecoach proprietors, but children might be encouraged to argue a case in their favour. One of the passengers did so, but he was a coach proprietor!

Plainly, the evidence these extracts provide gives scope for contextualising local findings about stagecoach journeys. It should be remembered, however, that road travellers using stagecoaches did not always comment unfavourably on the journeys they undertook. Indeed, they could be complimentary.

Coping with the aftermath of the stagecoach accident

1. How well would the actions the stagecoach travellers considered taking have worked? Think of arguments for and against each action. Discuss the arguments and then write them down in the table below.

Action	Arguments for	Arguments against
Walking to Ambleside leaving the injured man and coachman behind.	*The injured man could be kept comfortable*	*All the other passengers would have had a lengthy walk.*
Sending the coachman for help at Ambleside, riding one of the horses without a saddle.	*The coachman could get to Ambleside relatively quickly by horse, barring further mishaps.*	*Help for the injured man would take a good deal of time.* *The coachman might have difficulty finding carriages because they were already booked by those at the Windermere regatta.*
Hiring carriages from a local farmer	*Finding local transport might be quicker than going to Ambleside for help. If so, the injured man would receive medical help more quickly.*	*There was no certainty that local farmers could provide suitable transport.*

2. Decide whether each policy was likely to have been

   (a) very successful (b) quite successful (c) not very successful.

3. Which do you think would have been the most successful policy? Say why.

   ....

   ....

Children will inevitably ask what happened to Sir George Head and his fellow passengers. The coachman eventually reappeared, along with 'a cavalcade of three or four carriages of different descriptions'. One was an open landau – a four-wheeled carriage fitted with a folding hood - and the others were 'tub gigs' – two-wheeled vehicles pulled by a single horse. The injured man was laid full length along one of the seats in the landau and the rest of the passengers and their luggage rode in the tub gigs. The journey into Ambleside took about an hour. The injured man was attended to by a surgeon and, after a three-hour delay whilst arrangements were made, the tub gigs continued to Kendal without further mishap. They arrived at ten o'clock in the evening and the passengers found comfortable accommodation at an inn.

Teaching approaches linking local visual sources

As the stagecoach exercise shows, linking visual with written evidence can prove highly revealing about aspects of local history. So, too, can exercises that link local visual sources together. These exercises can be divided into the following types:

Then and now visuals

Providing children with a photograph of a local scene in the past along with a present-day photograph taken from the same vantage point, or as near as possible to it, enables them to consider continuities and changes over time. In exercises of this type, a two-stage approach may be preferred. The children begin by examining the older image, perhaps guided by questions of the type given above. They might work in groups, making factual and inferential observations. They then examine the newer image, noting key changes that have occurred, as well as continuities. They make lists of their findings. Class discussion might then take place to review the findings and to consider the reasons for the changes and the impact they have had. Features that often stand out on street-scene photographs of the late 19th and early 20th centuries are horse-drawn vehicles, perhaps with evidence of the street pollution they caused; shop window blinds; trams and tramlines; men as well as women wearing hats; and street surfaces formed from setts (blocks of stone cut to regular size and shape).[88] Robert Unwin has suggested that children might start an exercise of this type by considering which photograph is the older, listing the reasons on which their choice is based. They could then ask their own questions about the change and continuity they identify and assess whether they think the changes they observe have been for the better or worse.[89]

Where the comparison of images reveals demolition of buildings, or major alterations to them, discussion might be introduced on the criteria that children think should be used in terms of preserving buildings, including those in their own localities. They could be asked for examples, giving reasons for their selection. They might also consider whether they think that the changes revealed by the comparison have brought improvements.[90] There is scope, too, for children to

88 Setts are often confused with cobbles. Both were used to surface roads and paths, but cobbles are smooth stones of irregular shape and size, often taken from river beds or sea shores.

89 R. Unwin, *The Visual Dimension in the Study and Teaching of History* (Historical Association Teaching History Series, 49, 1981), pp.21-5.

90 A good example showing changes made to The Black Gate at Newcastle can be found in M.

discuss how visual material is presented. Thus old photographs of street scenes tend to be taken when the sun is shining (or at least when the weather is fine) and when the streets are busy with traffic and pedestrians. Positive images usually prevail.

Family photographs

The role that family history can play in key stage 1 provision is noted in chapter 4, emphasising the opportunity that arises for children to sequence family events. What can be added here is a reminder that photographs showing different generations of family members can add another dimension to this type of exercise. It is likely that family photographs will cover at least three generations.

Clearly, too, family photographs have a then and now dimension. They can be of further help in engaging children with the concept of continuity and change, most notably, perhaps, as far as fashions in clothing are concerned. But they may well be revealing in terms of several aspects of family life in the past, including holiday activities and venues; weddings and other celebrations; the houses family members occupied; their possessions; and the pets they kept.

Then and then visuals

Apart from enabling past to be compared with present, visual sources can be used to compare two or more periods in the past. Photographs of family life and street scenes may permit such comparisons, but the approach probably has the greatest use as far as maps are concerned. Thus exercises dealing with the theme of settlement growth might use map evidence from varying periods to help in showing the nature and extent of development. In Yorkshire and Lancashire, for example, six-inch to the mile Ordnance Survey maps can be particularly helpful in examining the growth of towns and of villages during the Victorian period.

There may also be possibilities for the evidence provided in paintings or engravings to be checked against contemporary photographs. At issue here is artistic licence. It may be the case, too, that different types of contemporaneous visuals can complement one another, enabling a fuller interpretation to be achieved.

Other teaching approaches using visual sources

An article by Jane Card discusses the appeal of visual images and why they stimulate thought, as well as describing part of a lesson with year 7 children based on class discussion of a visual source. She stresses the need to give children time to respond to the questions asked.[91] Alan Hodkinson has provided a useful division into closed, open, interpretive and evaluative questions that can be used in working with visual sources, as well as a case study of work arising from children scrutinising a photograph of a local Victorian slum scene.[92] Additionally, Tim

Mills, 'Turn your pupils into history detectives: using sources to interpret old photographs', *Primary History*, 38 (Winter, 2004), p.34.

91 J. Card, 'Talking pictures: exploiting the potential of visual sources to generate productive pupil talk', *Teaching History*,148 (September, 2012), pp.40-6.

92 A. Hodkinson, 'Using the visual image in primary schools: a beginners guide', *Primary History*, 49 (Summer, 2008), pp.14-15.

Lomas has reported a set of prompts that one school has devised to help children make use of visual evidence. He advises, too, on the ways in which visual sources can be used in the classroom.[93] Mention should also be made of Jacqui Dean's approach to structuring questions that can be asked of visual images. She delineates content; structure; message; time; situation; reason; and meaning.[94]

93 T. Lomas, 'History co-ordinators' dilemma: pedagogy and the visual image', *Primary History*, 49 (Summer, 2008), pp.10-11. The same volume of *Primary History* includes other articles dealing with using visual images in teaching. That written by John Fines offers advice on introducing visual images in the classroom.

94 J. Dean, 'The power of the visual image in learning: the Nuffield Primary History approach', *Primary History*, 49 (Summer, 2008), pp.22-3.

Chapter 8
Family life in the 1950s

Information about the lives of local families in the comparatively recent past can be obtained by listening to, and recording, the observations of adults about their life experiences, including those of childhood. Such activity can provide detailed and varied evidence that, when combined with other types of source material, can greatly facilitate the investigations into local history that children undertake.[95]

One means of obtaining information from previous generations about their experiences is to use short questionnaires. Compared with recording voices directly, these have advantage in generating evidence quickly and easily, with children for the most part noting the responses they obtain in tick-box form. The main part of this chapter is devoted to discussing this approach, using examples of recording sheets relating to aspects of family life in the 1950s, particularly as experienced by children. The concluding part of the chapter draws attention to other approaches children have used in gathering oral testimony as part of their local history studies, highlighting learning and teaching issues that arise.

Sheet content and rationale

Examples of recording sheets that can be used to gather oral testimony are given below. They cover the themes of home entertainment; family food; kitchen equipment; and playing outdoors. In each of the sheets, twelve items are included. Several of them would not have featured in family life during the 1950s, whereas, in some instances at least, the others would. The number of items included on the sheets can vary, but a reasonable balance between those that would and would not have featured helps in dealing with the notions of continuity and change. The point here is that the children can use their findings to compare aspects of their childhood with those of an older generation. In so doing, they can discuss the nature of changes that have occurred, as well as the causes and impact. With regard to entertainment and kitchen equipment, for instance, the influence of technological innovation can be considered, noting the new types of products that have become available. As far as food is concerned, the findings might reveal a greater variety in the takeaways that families buy, a trend that can be linked with the theme of people on the move. The findings might well give prompts from which

95 Plenty of general guidance is available on implementing oral history in schools, including the pitfalls to avoid. See, for example, S. Purkis, *Oral History in Schools* (Oral History Society, no date); A. Redfern, *Taking in Class: Oral History and the National Curriculum* (1996) and the same author's 'Oral history in primary schools', *Primary History*, 23 (October,1999) pp.14-16; I. Cramer, 'Oral history: working with children', *Teaching History*, 71 (April, 1993), pp.11-19; H. Claire, 'Oral History: a powerful tool or a double-edged sword?', *Primary History*, 38 (Winter, 2004), pp.20-3; and M. L. Parsons, 'Let's grab a granny off the street: the problems of oral history and how they can be minimalised', *Teaching History*, 84 (June, 1996), pp.30-3.

Examples of recording sheets

Home entertainment in the 1950s

Which did you have in your home in the 1950s?	Yes or no
colour television set	......
black and white television set	......
radio	......
computer games	......
tape recorder	......
record player	......
comics	......
compact disc player	......
board games	......
piano	......
card games	......
dominos	......

Please make any other comments

....

....

Family food in the 1950s

Which of these foods did you eat in the 1950s?	Yes or no
bought fish and chips	......
Chinese takeaways	......
Indian takeaways	......
ice cream	......
takeaway pizzas	......
lasagne	......
frozen peas	......
fish fingers	......
beef burgers	......
sausages	......
baked beans	......
tinned fruit	......

Please make any other comments

....

....

Kitchen equipment in the 1950s

Which of these did you have in your home in the 1950s?	Yes or no
gas cooker	......
electric cooker	......
microwave cooker	......
kitchen range	......
refrigerator	......
freezer	......
stainless steel sink	......
fitted kitchen cupboards	......
food mixer	......
dish washer	......
washing machine	......

Please make any other comments

....

....

Playing outdoors in the 1950s

Which of the following did you play with outdoors in the 1950s?	Yes or no
skateboard	......
bicycle	......
mountain bike	......
skipping rope	......
ball games	......
roller skates	......
roller blades	......
kite	......
football	......
cricket	......
hopscotch	......
tennis	......

Please state your gender .... and make other comments if you wish.

....

....

further discussion can emerge. Thus consideration of developments in takeaway eating could lead to discussion on the rise of convenience foods. The rise of 'TV dinners' might also be aired.

Some themes lend themselves to additional analysis. In investigating outdoor games, for example, the differing preferences of boys and girls might be addressed. Accordingly, space has been made on the recording form for respondents to state their gender. Other themes can be explored, of course, as can other time periods. Holidays during the 1950s are one possibility, offering opportunity to consider changes over time in destinations, activities and means of transport. Shopping practices is another, bringing in such developments as buying online, going to supermarkets and purchasing with a credit or debit card.

Senior family members and acquaintances who grew up in the locality, which can be broadly defined geographically, can provide respondents. Investigation might take place with groups of children assuming responsibility for different aspects of the family life theme. If each child in the class obtains just one or two completed response sheets, more than sufficient information will be obtained. The point of the exercise is not to generate vast amounts of evidence, even though this could be useful, but rather to lead children to gather evidence that will promote their historical understanding. In other words, they will be actively engaged in purposeful learning, with the added advantage that they are actually generating historical evidence. And their respondents can remain anonymous.

Space is also made on the sheets for recording additional comment from the respondents, so that open as well as closed responses can be generated. Either the children or the respondents could write down these comments. More space for this purpose can be usefully included on the sheets than is shown in the examples, though brief comment is all that is required. Such comment can provide details about individual experiences that not only add a great deal of interest to the exercise, but also give valuable insights into prevailing practices and attitudes that help to explain the findings. Thus, when the sheets were trialled, one male respondent to the home entertainment sheet remarked:

> Comics weren't allowed in the house, only books. My parents believed that comics created lazy readers. There was no television in the house until after I left the house in 1965. The record player was a radiogram, which only my father was allowed to use. I had no records until I had my own record player in 1965.[96]

This evidence also brings advantage because it reveals that whilst playing records took place in the respondent's home, it did so on a restricted basis and not necessarily with the preferences of all family members being taken into account. Two other respondents noted that their families bought television sets in 1953 to watch the coronation of Elizabeth II.

96 The respondent was in his early twenties when he left home.

On the subject of playing outdoors, one respondent stated that he played out for 90 per cent of the time, whilst another, also male, commented:

> I saved up £2 to buy an ancient bicycle. I rubbed it down and repainted it myself. I was 10 years old ... My roller skates very were important to me. What I really wanted to do was ice skate, but there was no chance of that.

These observations invite discussion about how far children have moved from playing outdoors and from restoring second-hand possessions, a matter which could be linked with the wartime slogan of 'make do and mend'.

Using the evidence

Group work might be used so children can pool their findings and report them to the rest of the class. The returns might also be collated for analysis and presented in bar graph form, as in the example shown below. It is based on a survey of ten people who were children during the 1950s.

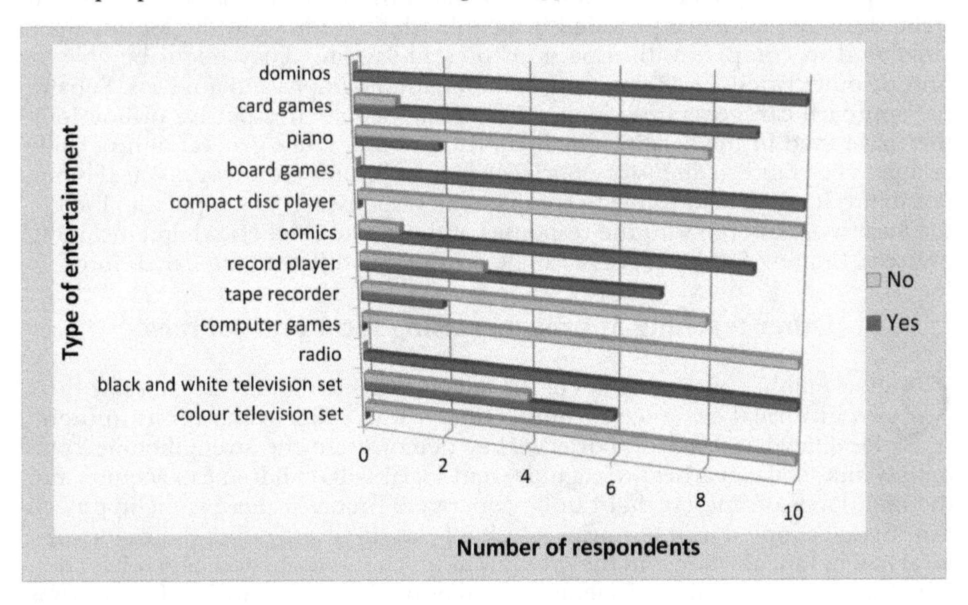

Creating charts of this type obviously gives children useful practice in creating spreadsheets and presenting numerical data in effective ways. However, the charts are not ends in themselves and children will need guidance in drawing and stating conclusions based on them. As Ruth Noall has pointed out, spreadsheet graphs help children to interpret statistical evidence by revealing patterns and relationships, but do not explain the form they take. Accordingly, more detailed interpretation requires teacher discussion and perhaps further research.[97]

As intended from the items included in the recording sheet, the findings shown in the chart should suggest to children that radios, dominoes and board games were likely to have been generally available as home entertainments in the 1950s, along

97 R. Noall, 'How can the use of spreadsheets enhance children's learning in history: a case study', *Primary History*, 26 (October, 2000), pp.16-17.

with board games and comics, whilst colour television sets, compact disc players and computer games would not have been. Children should also be able to appreciate that pianos, tape recorders and record players were all available, but the indications are that by no means all households had them. Differing household incomes could well have been influential here. But so, too, may household preferences, as the comments about comics noted above reveal.

Matters arising

The limited size of samples obtained from distributing the questionnaire sheets only becomes an issue if attempts are made to generalise from them about the extent to which certain items were used in the 1950s. Black and white television sets and record players are examples. Obtaining evidence from previous generations, either in oral or written form, certainly gives valuable insights into the diversity of individual experience. Yet it does raise concerns about representativeness and hence of the need to be guarded in making generalisations based upon it.

The approach adopted in the exercise could contribute to a local study in its own right, using the evidence provided by people who have lived in the locality since childhood to compare with aspects of present-day life. They might be able to provide other types of evidence, too, including photographs and artefacts. Equally, the approach can generate evidence from local people, irrespective of how long they have lived in the locality, which contributes to a more general unit of study relating to recent Britain history. Social change in Britain since World War II is one possibility. It might be possible to compare the responses from people who lived in the locality as children with the responses of those who lived elsewhere, including overseas. Context for the exercise can be provided in different ways, therefore.

Other teaching approaches using local oral sources

Quite a number of case studies of the ways in which children can generate their own historical evidence through contact with older generations in their localities have been reported. They demonstrate the strengthening community links that can arise; the cognitive and social skills children can acquire; and the high levels of interest that can be generated. Amongst them is the approach Tina Sudell adopted with her primary school class in investigating the history of a local hall in Lincolnshire and the grounds in which it was situated. She relates that the project was initiated after a letter written by one of the children in her class was published in a local newspaper. The letter asked for people who had worked at the hall, or who had other connections with it, to make contact. As a result, several letters were received describing life in and around the hall as it was remembered between the 1920s and 1940s. In developing the project, respondents were invited to spend an afternoon in the school to answer questions from small groups of children. The approach helped to give children a sense of ownership in undertaking the project and cross-curricular dimensions emerged. An impressive example of one child's work is reproduced in the account of the project.[98]

An article by Mick Anderson also deals with bringing respondents into school, in his case a war veteran. He stresses the need to place the evidence obtained from

98 T. Sudell, 'Let's adopt a monument: a school's approach to covering history, literacy, science, and citizenship in an interesting way', *Primary History,* 22 (April, 1999), pp.18-21.

oral testimony in a wider context.[99] War veterans and local people who lived through World War II were also the interviewees in a project at Hemel Hempstead undertaken by Lynda Abbot and Richard Grayson. The project was devised as an extra-curricular activity and was undertaken by 14-18 year olds. The local branch of the Royal British Legion helped to identify interviewees. A wide range of issues was covered in the interviews, but, above all, those concerned were able to appreciate the huge disruption that World War II had on their community and how the entire community became involved in the war effort.[100] A project devised by Paul Barrett for year 9 children also addressed the impact of World War II, in this case on New Milton in Hampshire.[101] His approach, which demonstrates the value that studying family history can have at secondary level, centred on children investigating the involvement of their own families in the war, with the aim of deepening their appreciation of the diverse experiences that occurred. The project was set within the context of a broader historical enquiry on aspects of the war and built on the tradition of inviting grandparents into the school to work with year 7 children.

Another approach, considered in an article written by Jill Watson and Penelope Harnett, involved a group of children obtaining oral testimony by visiting an old persons' home. The authors give advice on preparing children to conduct interviews effectively.[102] Rather than visiting respondents at their own homes or at residential homes, Peter Rogers suggests attending their social gatherings, making arrangements through the voluntary organisations involved.[103] Thorough preparation in interviewing and recording skills, including the use of camcorders, is again evident in a project called *Exploring Our Roots.* Based in several Manchester secondary schools and led by Jackie Ould-Okojie, the project involved children gathering oral testimony about the experiences of migration and settlement in Manchester. A key aim of the project was to foster relationships between each contributing school and its main ethnic minority community. A teaching pack was produced, organised on a thematic basis.[104]

Some oral history projects have dealt with unusual local history themes. For example, *Up the Manor!* took as its broad focus the history of sport in east London. Led by Michelle Johansen and Martin Spafford, the project involved an ethnically-diverse group of year 10 boys interacting with a set of exclusively white men who were formerly members of a local boys' club.[105] Another example, devised by Chris

99 M. Anderson, 'Oral history: a source of evidence for children in the primary classroom', *Primary History*, 55 (Summer, 2010), pp.32-3.

100 L. Abbot and R. S. Grayson, 'Community engagement in local history: a report on the Hemel at War project', *Teaching History*, 145 (December, 2012), pp.4-12.

101 P. Barrett, '"My grandfather slammed the door in Winston Churchill's face!": using family history to provoke rigorous enquiry', *Teaching History*, 145 (December, 2011), pp.14-21.

102 J. Watson and P. Harnett, 'What was it like when you were at school?', *Primary History*, 15 (February,1997), pp.10-12.

103 P. Rogers, '"Silver linings": using the elderly as a resource', *Primary History*, 10 (June 1995), pp.14-15.

104 J. Ould-Okojie, 'Exploring our roots: oral history in the local community', *Primary History*, 46 (Summer, 2007), pp.18-19.

105 M. Johansen and M. Spafford, '"How our area used to be back then: an oral history

Edwards, involved children from years 7 to 9 at a Stoke Newington school in an investigation of 'Yob Culture'. They addressed the question 'were children in the past more respectful of authority than children today?'. The end products were a computer-based oral history archive and a radio history documentary.[106]

In her evaluation of an oral history project she undertook with rural primary schools in Cumbria, Dylis Evans raised several issues. They include the comment made by some respondents that they would have liked to have seen the questionnaire that was used prior to the interview taking place. The matter of allowing respondents time to think beforehand, perhaps clarifying memories with others, arises. She also remarks that close questioning impeded some of the respondents, but did allow children to compare and contrast.[107] Plainly, a balance needs to be struck.

project in an east London school', *Teaching History*,134 (March, 2009), pp.37-46.

106 C. Edwards, 'Putting life into history: how pupils can use oral history to become critical historians', *Teaching History*, 123 (June, 2006), pp.21-5.

107 D. Evans, 'A small oral history project in four rural Cumbrian primary schools', *Teaching History*, 57 (October, 1989), pp.25-7.

Chapter 9
Changes in Victorian terraced houses

In extending discussion on using physical evidence in teaching local history, this chapter turns to possibilities offered by the built environment. It begins with an exercise based on observing the features of small terraced houses. These became a characteristic form of housing for ordinary families during the 19th century and though demolition has taken its toll, a great deal of it survives. Most of it dates from the three or four decades leading up to World War I, but earlier examples can still be found, commonly in rural areas. Making use of the evidence that this type of housing affords is invaluable in helping children to investigate aspects of local domestic life over the period and the ways in which the housing standards for at least some ordinary families improved.[108]

Consideration is also given to the ways in which children's investigations into these matters can be extended with the use of documentary evidence. Emphasis is on the rather unwholesome topic of domestic sanitation, making particular use of evidence derived from large-scale maps and public health reports. Finally, other ways in which children can use the built environment in their local history investigations are considered, emphasising the nature of the evidence that it provides.

General observations

Either through field observation, or, at least in part, using photographs, children can compare the frontages of small terraced houses built during the early decades of the 19th century with those built during the late 19th or early 20th centuries. They can concentrate on the differences in order to examine the type of changes that took place over time. In doing so, they will have to infer and, accordingly, to be aware of uncertainties. Moreover, as John Fines stresses, they will need to be taught to observe closely, taking careful notes of their findings.[109]

To illustrate the approach, the photographs of house frontages shown below can be considered. The earlier houses are situated in Liverpool Road, Hutton, a rural area near Preston in Lancashire, and the later ones in Murray Street, Preston. There are no date-stones on the houses, but those at Hutton are shown on a six-inch Ordnance Survey map of the mid-1840s, when Murray Street was still undeveloped. In several respects, including the minimum height of domestic rooms, the Murray Street houses conformed to building regulations that came into effect in Preston during the mid-1870s; they are probably late Victorian houses, therefore.

---

108 Background reading for teachers that will help with developing children's investigations into aspects of housing history include J. Burnett, *A Social History of Housing, 1815-1970* (Methuen, 1978); S. Muthesius, *The English Terraced House* (Yale University Press, 1982); and R. Rodger, *Housing in Urban Britain, 1780-1914* (MacMillan, 1989).

109 J. Fines, 'Doing local history', *Primary History*, 55 (Summer, 2010), pp.6-7.

Liverpool Road, Hutton. Murray Street, Preston.

Working in groups or as a whole class, children can be challenged to spot differences between the rows of houses in the following respects:

- the heights of the houses;
- front garden provision;
- whether or not there is a fanlight over the front door;
- amount of architectural decoration;
- numbers of chimney pots per stack;
- differences in the way the bricks are laid.

Several points arise in relation to these matters:

1 The upstairs windows in the older row of houses are less deep than those in the later houses; in the later houses upper and lower windows are of equal depth. In fact, the later houses are taller than the earlier ones. The point here is that, during the Victorian period, building regulations imposed by local landowners and by the enactment of local bye-laws, stipulated a minimum height for rooms in new houses.

2 The older houses have front gardens, whereas those in the town do not. The cost of building land would have been influential here. However, late 19th and early 20th century terraced houses built on town outskirts often have gardens.

3 Provision of a fanlight shows that the later houses had a vestibule (inner porch) or lobby (hallway). Greater privacy arose as a result, not least when visitors arrived

and the front door was opened to them. Draughts and heat loss might also be reduced by having an inner door.

4 The older houses have a plain external appearance, with little in the way of decoration. However, the lintels are splayed, that is they slope at the ends. There is more decoration on the later houses, including chamfered window lintels and projecting cornices in the door lintels.

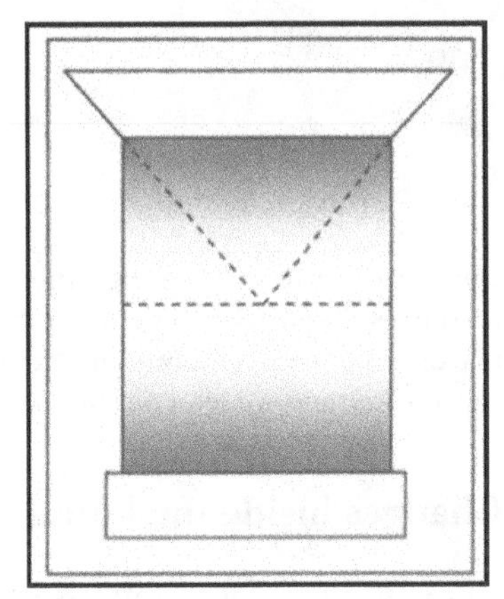

As this illustration shows, the slope at the ends of splayed window lintels is determined by an imaginary horizontal line running through the centre of the window.

5 The number of chimney pots per chimney stack indicates the number of fireplaces in each house. If each of the houses had four rooms – the ubiquitous two-up two-down house – then each room in the later houses could have had a fireplace. However, a complication arises where, as in the case of the earlier houses, there are four rooms but, as was the case originally, just two chimney pots per stack. Assuming all the chimney pots and their associated flues served open fireplaces, six possibilities arise as to which were the two rooms that could be heated. These are

- the two upstairs;
- the two downstairs;
- the two front;
- the two back;
- the back downstairs and front upstairs;
- the back upstairs and front downstairs

Children can vote on the matter, offering reasons for their choice. Read on for the answer!

6 The manner in which the bricks are laid (or bonded) generally reveals whether or not cavity walls were provided. The older houses have solid walls with the bricks laid in English garden wall bonding. The newer houses have cavity walls shown by stretcher bonding.[110]

110 The other common type of brick bonding is Flemish bonding. Alternate headers and stretchers are laid both vertically and horizontally. Considered more decorative than English garden wall bonding, it is often found on larger houses and public buildings. For further

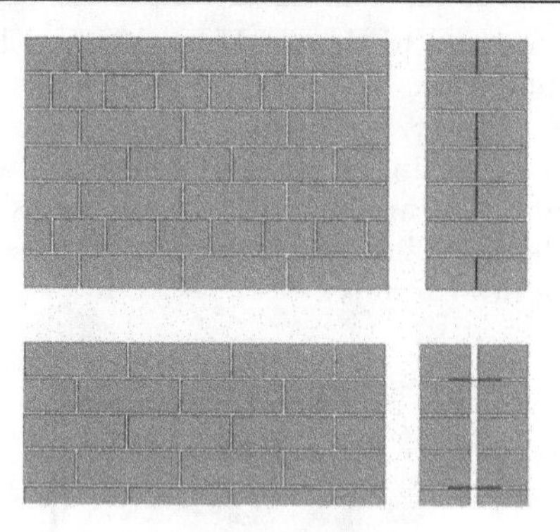

Brick bonding.

Top example: English garden wall bonding. In most courses, the sides of the brick are exposed (stretcher rows), but every few courses, the bricks go through the wall so that their ends are exposed (header rows). Bottom example: Stretcher bonding. No bricks go through the wall, so a cavity can be made to stop damp penetration. Metal ties link outer and inner walls.

Changes inside the house

The illustrations below show the type of layout associated with the early- and late-19th century houses. They reveal more about the changes made to them.

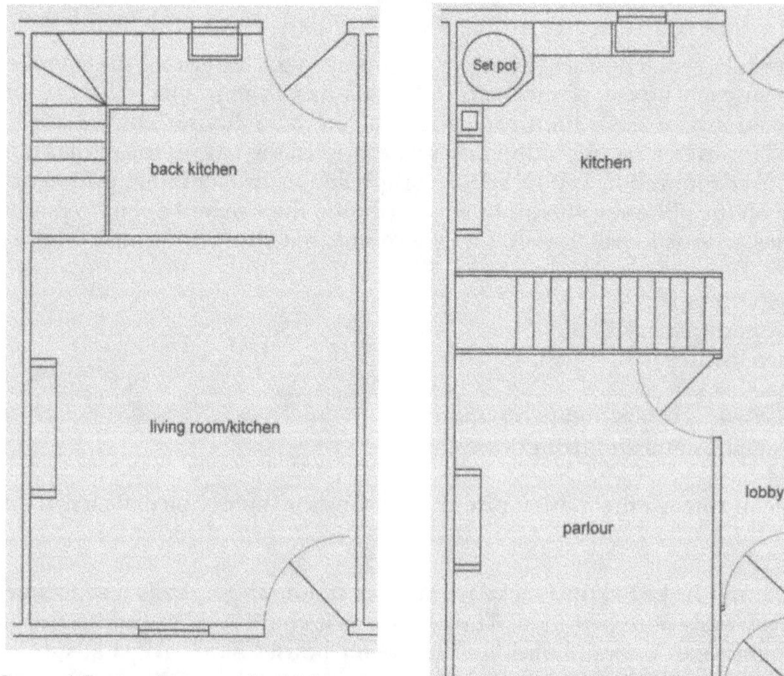

Ground-floor plans: early 19th century house (L) and late 19th century house (R)

details, see R. Brunskill and A. Clifton-Taylor, *English Brickwork* (Ward Lock, 1977).

Turning first to the chimney pot issue, children might well reason that the two downstairs rooms would be heated, since the kitchen (at the back) would require a fire for cooking and the living room (at the front) would require a fire to keep family members warm in cold weather. However, as the ground-floor plan of the early 19th century house reveals, the downstairs rear room did not have a fireplace. Referred to as a back kitchen or a scullery, this room contained the stairs and a slop stone – a shallow sink used for washing. The front room comprised a living room/ kitchen and occupied a greater space than the back kitchen. It was here that family life centred.

Comparison of the ground-floor plans enables children to see the type of changes that occurred in working-class houses over the Victorian era. They include:

- Provision of more fireplaces, adding to the comfort of living in the houses.
- Making the front room into a parlour by adding an internal lobby. The parlour gave a more private room that tended to be used for receiving special visitors and for important family occasions.
- Providing a set pot in the kitchen, as well as a fireplace. Sometimes referred to as a copper, but normally made from cast iron, set pots were heated by a coal fire, the flue of which is shown in the plan. Set pots provided boiling water in which white cloth items could be washed.[111]
- Making the kitchen occupy a larger proportion of the downstairs space and positioning the stairs to occupy a more central location.

Matters arising

Small terraced houses built during the late 19th and early 20th centuries often show more architectural detail than the Murray Street examples. And blocks of houses within terraces can differ, being separated by straight joints.[112] They might also have single- or double-storey rear extensions and projecting windows at

Straight joints arise where a new building joins an existing one and the bricks or stones are not bonded together. As shown here, the brick courses in new and existing walls might not meet at quite the same height.

111 Examples of set pots can be seen at <http://www.1900s.org.uk/copper-water-heater.htm>.

112 The blocks might contain few houses, showing the stages in which they were built, and indicating that small-scale builders were operating.

the front. Additionally, walls made from rough-textured, hand-made bricks (which often contain small pieces of stone) gave way to smooth-textured, machine-made bricks. Yet some houses with kitchen/living room continued to be built.

The same type of changes occurred with houses built from stone. In the Pennine areas, water-shot coursing, in which the outer stones were laid at a slight outward tilt, seemingly so moisture could drain out, was commonly used from the late 18th to the mid-19th century.[113] Examples of the technique can be seen in the *Through the Valley of Stone* website at <http://www.valleyofstone.org.uk/journey/stoneinthelandscape/fashions>.

From around the mid-19th century, rock-faced stone blocks were used. These are squared so they fit together well, but the outer face is chiselled to give a rough, rock-like appearance.[114]

Census schedule evidence could be used to show the variation in household size that occurred in small terraced houses during Victorian times, leading to discussion on how large families coped. Sleeping accommodation was an issue, one strand of contemporary opinion arguing that separate sleeping arrangements should be provided for boys and girls. Occupational detail should indicate whether mothers had paid occupations and at what age children were likely to have started work; birth place information will provide insights into population movement. Working with a year 7 class and using 1881 and 1911 census schedules relating to houses in Wood Green, London, Amy Hughes and Heather De Silva have demonstrated the type of comparative household analysis that children can undertake.[115]

Context for this type of exercise could be provided by including it as part of a theme dealing with urban development in Britain during the 19th century, perhaps linking the provision of housing to factory development and hence the formation of 'industrial colonies'. Given the need to harness water for steam raising and condensing, urban factories were often located in river valleys and alongside canals. To appreciate this type of development, children might compare sections of photocopied Ordnance Survey maps from several neighbouring towns, along with photographs of some of the houses.

Developments in house sanitation

Children can also discover much about changes in local domestic sanitation during and beyond the Victorian era, particularly by using public health and medical officer of health reports. Thus, as noted in chapter 2, the extract from William Lee's 1851 report on the public health of Rotherham and Kimberworth mentions houses without privies, whilst those taken from the Stockport medical

113 Because water-shot coursing is often found only on the front walls of buildings, with random stonework to the rear and sides, it may have been in part incorporated because it was seen to be pleasing in appearance.

114 The blocks were chiselled from the sides slanting outwards towards the centre. See J. P. Allen, *Practical Building Construction* (Crosby Lockwood, 1900), p.69.

115 A. Hughes and H. De Silva, 'One Street, twenty children and the experience of a changing town: year 7 explore the story of a London street', *Teaching History*, 151 (June, 2013), pp.55-63. The children also used maps, photographs, field evidence and other sources.

officer of health reports for 1910 and 1914 detail several different types of 'closet accommodation', which, in some instances, were still being shared between two or more families.

One teaching approach is to provide children with brief source material extracts that enable them to trace the type of developments that occurred during this period, using the headings of open cesspit or midden privies; pail closets; back streets (or passages); and water-closets.

Open cesspit or midden privies

A start could be made by considering the nature of open cesspit privies.[116] These may be described in a sanitary report for the children's own locality. If not, evidence from elsewhere can be used, such as that contained in Charles Babbage's 1850 report on the public health of Haworth, the West Yorkshire village associated with the Bronte sisters.[117] Babbage found no sewers there and just a few drains running along gutters and open channels. He continued:

> As a necessary consequence of the want of sewerage there is contiguous to each privy a receptacle for the night soil, in some cases walled round, in other cases fenced in with upright stones on edge: into these midden-steads are thrown the household refuse and the offal from the slaughter houses, where, mixed with the night soil, and occasionally with the drainage from pigsties, the whole lies for months together, decomposition goes on and offensive smells and putrid gases are given out. These midden-steads are uncovered, and the majority were nearly full when I examined them. Bad as they are, their close proximity to dwelling-houses makes them much more injurious.

This type of extract could be read out to inform the class and promote discussion. For some towns, 1840s five feet to the mile Ordnance Survey maps can be used to show cesspit privies, as in the example below. A key point to note in this case is that access to several of the yards was via narrow passages between the houses. The contents of the privies had to be dug out and taken through the passages to the front of the houses for disposal, probably in a horse-drawn cart.[118] Improvement was achieved when each house had its own passage or shared a passage with the adjoining house.

116 The terms used by contemporaries varied.

117 Extracts from the report can be viewed online at <https://www.bl.uk/collection-items/sanitary-report-on-haworth-home-to-the-bronts>.

118 The disposal of night-soil raises another area of local investigation for children that can be contextualised in relation to present-day practices. These practices may come as something of a surprise to both teacher and taught. Guidance in relation to the horticultural dimension of the issue can be found in an essay entitled 'Night soil and other euphemisms ... '. It forms part of the *Parks and Gardens UK* website at <https://parksandgardensuk.wordpress.com/about/>.

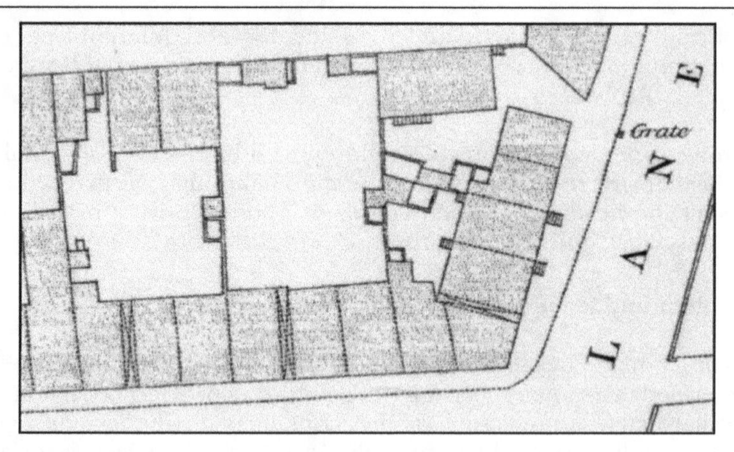

Source: 1840s five feet to the mile OS map of Chorley, Lancashire.

The houses and privies are shaded, whereas the open middens (or cesspits) adjoining the privies are unshaded. The yards varied in size and some privies were shared.

Pail closets

As the illustration below reveals, excreta was collected in pails located inside privies rather than being allowed to accumulate in open cesspits. One pail per privy became usual. Because a pail collected far less ordure than a cesspit, more regular emptying was required to ensure effective usage. The normal stipulation was that the pails should be emptied at night – hence the term night soil - so that, assuming

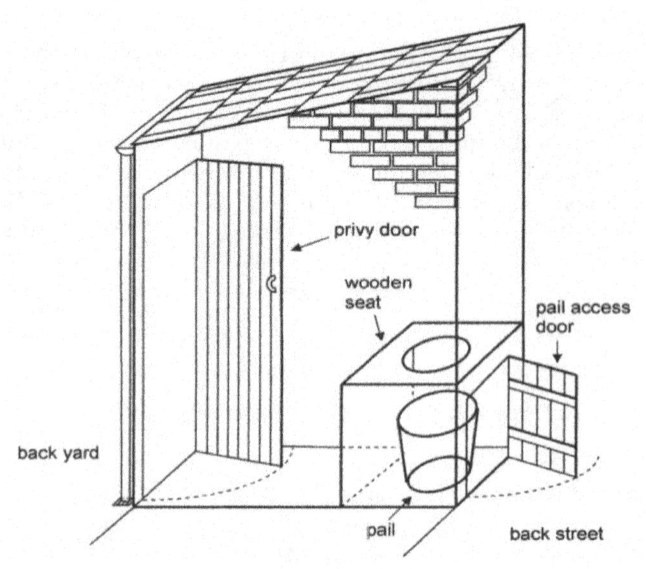

Pail-closet privy.

In this case, access to the pail was via a door at the rear of the privy. In other cases, there was no rear door and access to the pail was gained by lifting the wooden seat, which was hinged. The full pail was then carried out through the privy door. Clearly, providing a rear door saved much time and effort in emptying pails.

bedroom windows were closed, the impact of the offensive smells arising would be minimised. Spillage might occur during the emptying process, however, and the task might not always be completed before daybreak. Complaints could result. Children might deliberate on the degree of improvement that was achieved.

Back streets (or passages)

Examples of back streets are shown on the extract from the 25-inch to the mile Ordnance Survey map of Stockport, reproduced in chapter 3. They brought advantage in that pail closets could be serviced from the rear of houses instead of from the front. A good deal of time and effort could be saved as a result, especially if the privy was situated adjoining the passage and the passage was wide enough to accommodate a horse and cart, as in the case of the illustration shown below. Offensive smells at the front of the houses would also have been lessened, if not entirely eliminated.

Night-soil men at Colne in North-east Lancashire, c.1900.The illustration is reproduced by permission of Lancashire County Council.

They appear to be emptying ash bins as well as excreta tubs. An example of the latter can be seen just beyond the brush. The small door at ground-floor level just beyond the ashbin in the foreground gave access to an excreta tub. The small doorways at head-height level covered openings in the back walls of coal places. The bags of coal could be offloaded directly from carts.

Water-closets

As sewerage systems were constructed during Victorian times and beyond, domestic water-closets were increasingly installed. Medical officer of health reports give details of the progress made. Some were waste-water closets, also known as tipplers or tippers. An example is shown below. After the water in the slop stone - a form of sink - had been used, it was drained into the tipper. This was a hollow, earthenware vessel situated in the yard below ground level. Because it was pivoted, the tipper could swing freely and was so shaped that, when full of water, it automatically tipped over. As a result, a flush of water was discharged down the underground pipes to sweep away ordure that was deposited when the privy was used. The design of waste-water closets varied, the tipper sometimes being close to the privy and the pedestal or pan pipe beneath the privy seat being placed vertically.[119] As reservoirs were constructed, mains water could be used to flush away waste matter.

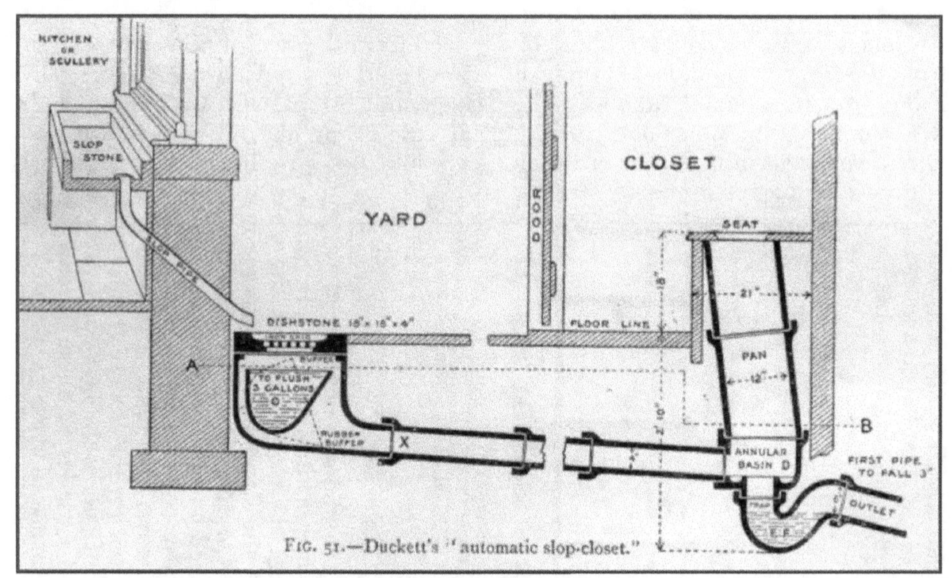

Fig. 51.—Duckett's "automatic slop-closet."

Source: J. L. Notter and R. H Firth, *Hygiene* (Longmans,1894), p.212.

The water trap situated beneath the base of the pedestal helped to reduce smells from the sewers. Rainwater from the yard could also enter the tipper.

Matters arising

Children might be introduced to the influences that brought about improvements in 19th century domestic sanitation. Growing amounts of statistical data on appalling levels of mortality, particularly amongst infants, provided ammunition for sanitary reformers to exert pressure locally. Securing local improvement acts was important in ensuring that advances could take place, whilst the 1875 Public Health Act stipulated that newly-built houses had to be provided with 'a sufficient watercloset earthcloset or privy'. Laying sewers and improving water supply by building reservoirs was essential in achieving reform, as were technological advances in water-closet design. Additionally, demand for better sanitary provision increased as the real incomes of at least some working-class families rose, hence enabling them to afford the relatively high rent levels that could be asked for better-quality houses.

Improvements in domestic sanitation might form part of a more general theme dealing with Victorian public health. A local case study might be developed,

119 A working tippler toilet can be seen at the Manchester Museum of Science and Industry.

contextualised by drawing on evidence from a group of local towns and/or villages.

Other approaches to local history using field evidence

The following are examples of the type of exercises involving the use of field evidence in which children might be involved. As with the Victorian housing example, linkage with documentary sources will help them to extend and deepen their investigations. The *Nuffield Primary History Project* offers useful advice in undertaking local history fieldwork, including dealing with permission and safety issues and making problem solving a central feature of the work that children undertake on site.[120]

More housing studies

At an early stage, children could become familiar with different types of dwellings in their locality – terraced, detached, bungalow, flat and so on – as well as the materials from which they were built, perhaps examining fragments of building materials - brick, stone, concrete, slate and so on. They might experiment to discover the qualities of these materials and hence their suitability for building purposes. That slate is waterproof and could be cut thinly made it useful as a roofing material, for example. It may be possible to take photographs of local houses built at various times in the past, including a very recent one, so that children can observe them to gain a sense of how house features have changed over time. They might use the photographs in a sequencing exercise.

Children might also investigate local houses built for the better off. Large terraced dwellings erected in or near to town centres during the 18th and 19th centuries, sometimes surrounding squares, are possibilities. They might note that these houses are often several stories high, with kitchen basements lit by windows projecting above ground floor level and hence requiring steps to the front door. Attic rooms were usual, too. The basement space would have been the province of servants, as would attic bedrooms. Blocked or 'blind' windows might be found, which may have had more to do with providing architectural detail than avoiding the window tax; the room with the blocked window may have a glazed window and would not have needed another. The association of these houses with classical revival architecture might also be addressed, a matter that is considered below. Teaching resources relating to a middle-class square in Leeds can be found in the *Urban Spaces* component of the Nuffield Primary History Project. Guidance is given on fieldwork and follow-up classroom resources. Details can be found at <https://www.history.org.uk/primary/categories/local-study?page=3>.

Residential suburbs for the better-off that emerged in many areas during the Victorian period might also be studied, building on the comments made in chapter 4. Children might discover that the houses in these suburbs are often detached or semi-detached rather than terraces; that they have sizeable garden areas; and that they may be set in curvilinear streets. They might also discover that, with more building space available, the inconvenience of basement kitchens and front door steps could be avoided. Class discussion might take place on the healthier and

120 Nuffield Primary History Project, 'Local history field work – top ten pointers for success', *Primary History*, 55 (Summer, 2010), p.15.

more private living space that these suburbs brought, though they were located at a distance from town centre facilities. Large-scale Ordnance survey maps add greatly to field evidence children can use to investigate suburban development. Some Victorian residential suburbs were linked with the formation of freehold land societies. These enabled working men to make regular subscriptions for the purchase of freehold land and the voting rights that went with it. An article by Robin Coulthard and Roy Patterson describes the work undertaken by three year 6 girls into the history of a freehold land housing estate in Darlington.[121]

Guidance for teachers on using the evidence derived from earlier housing can be found in a case study of timber-framed buildings erected at Ledbury, in Hertfordshire, during Tudor times. Part of the Victoria County History's *Schools Learning Zone* resources, the case study is designed for key stage two pupils to work in groups. The resources include details of a fieldtrip to view the external features of the town's Tudor houses; of a visit to Ledbury church to view the memorial to one of the town's wealthiest Tudor families; and investigation of the transcribed wills, with bequests, that several of Ledbury's Tudor townsmen left. The resources can be viewed at <http://www.victoriacountyhistory.ac.uk/schools/content/teaching-material.html>.

Architectural detail

Children could investigate the way in which revived classical styles of architecture – those developed in ancient Greece and Rome - have been used in local buildings erected during the last few centuries, churches included. Features such as columns, pediments and rounded arches might be considered, along with the symmetry and proportion of frontages. They might also examine medieval styles of architecture in the locality. These are characterised by pointed arches and are particularly associated with churches. Some examples date back to medieval times, but many others date from the 19th century when medieval (or Gothic) styles were also revived. Children might be introduced to the differing periods and styles of pointed architecture - Early English, decorated and perpendicular – showing their understanding by preparing annotated displays. These could go into some detail, noting, for example, the quatrefoil and dagger motifs that feature in the tracery of church windows built in the decorated style.[122] Appreciating why local historic buildings take a particular form and the impact they had, or still have, on the built environment can lead children into consideration of, and involvement in, conservation and redevelopment issues, thereby linking with the citizenship agenda.[123]

121 R. Coulthard and R. Patterson, 'History through streets', *Primary History*, 12, (November, 1996), pp. 6-8.

122 Particularly helpful guidance with this type of work can be found in the volumes of Nikolaus Pevsner's *Buildings of England* series. They provide architectural details, including a standard glossary of terms, for all localities in Britain. For some areas, both original and revised volumes are available. *Looking at Buildings* is a web site linked to the Pevsner guides, dealing with such matters as architectural terms and styles, building materials and types of buildings. Sections of the site are devoted to architectural studies of Birmingham, Bristol, Leeds, Liverpool, London, Manchester and Sheffield. The site is at <http://www.lookingatbuildings.org.uk/index.html>. Useful, too, is C. D. Cragoe, *How To Read Buildings: A Crash Course in Architecture* (Bloomsbury Publishing, 2008).

123 See, for example, M. Corbishley, 'Our heritage: use it or lose it', *Primary History*, 51

Studies of local architecture can be linked with a long-term housing theme by studying the change from vernacular to polite forms. The former feature local materials and building styles, with function being seen to be more important than appearance. The latter are associated with materials and styles that can be drawn from outside the locality and appearance assumes high importance.[124] The extent of change from vernacular to polite forms varies, a matter on which children can be challenged to make judgements. Locally-quarried stone, say, might still be used in building Victorian houses that are notable for their ornate appearance.

Roads, canals and railways

In most localities, children can inform their studies of transport developments by drawing on field evidence. One task is to determine how contemporaries grappled with gradient, a vital matter for all forms of transport. With canals, of course, completely flat stretches of water had to be created. This was partly achieved by taking circuitous routes around hillsides, with locks being provided to access different levels. Some cutting into the hillside would be required to create a ledge along which the canal could run. The hillside formed one side of the canal; the other side was formed by embankments, made at least in part from the material dug out of the hillside. Narrow tunnels were also made and valleys crossed by double-sided embankments and by constructing aqueducts.[125] Children could consider how barges were propelled through tunnels, since towpaths for horses were not provided.[126]

With roads and railways, the issue for children to appreciate is that contemporary engineers sought to achieve as gentle inclines as possible, bearing in mind the costs involved. In doing so, they used the same sort of techniques as the canal engineers. However, railway companies had far bigger sums of money available than canal companies or turnpike trusts, so they were able to undertake earth works on a much greater scale. And road builders had to ease gradients on both new and existing roads. The need to do so became greater as industrialisation intensified in Britain during the 18th and 19th centuries and an ever-rising volume of horse-drawn goods and passenger traffic was generated. Road builders aimed at achieving gradients no steeper than about 1 in 30. In addition to forming cuttings and embankments, often supported by retaining walls, they reduced the summit height of roads; constructed by-passes to avoid steep hills; and raised the heights of bridges in valley bottoms. Evidence of these techniques is likely to be found in most localities.

(Spring, 2008), pp.8-9 and G. Clemitshaw, 'Have we got the question right? Engaging future citizens in local history enquiry', *Teaching History*, 106 (March, 2002), pp.20-7.

124 For an introduction to the theme, see R. W. Brunskill, *Traditional Buildings of Britain: An Introduction to Vernacular Architecture and Its Revival* (Cassell, third edition, 2004).

125 Advice on visits to local canal sites, including preparation and on-site activities, can be found in T. Pickford, 'On the canal', *Primary History*, 5 (November, 1993), pp.9-11.

126 A plank was placed across the front part of the barge. Two men lay on their backs on the plank, their legs reaching to opposite sides of the tunnel. They then walked along the sides of the tunnel. They had to do so at the same pace in order to keep the barge at an even distance from the sides. The process was known as 'legging'.

Gravestones and war memorials

Local places of worship and of memorials to the deceased in graveyards and cemeteries can be highly instructive as sources of historical evidence. An exercise devised by Thelma Wiltshire involved year 6 children in noting features at St Grwst church, Llanwrst. In viewing the features as historical evidence, the children had to decide whether they could make factual statements (the evidence 'tells') or statements that were based on inference or speculation (the evidence 'suggests').[127] Hilary Cooper has provided a range of questions and activities with which children at key stages 1 and 2 can engage in relation to the features they can observe in local churches, whilst she and Pat Etched have reported work undertaken by key stage 1 children on a visit to a church in Kendal.[128] Rubbings made of gravestone inscriptions featured in the tasks the children undertook. Kenneth Lindsey provides guidance on how gravestone rubbings can be made. His book deals with other aspects of gravestones that children can study, including the materials from which they are made; the inscriptions on them; and the signs and symbols they display.[129] Bev Forrest notes how children can use memorials in cemeteries to gain insights into such matters as Victorian family life, local occupations and migration into and from the locality. Her article also describes investigations undertaken at a local cemetery by year 5 children at Ireland Wood primary school in Leeds, along with their follow-up work on family history.[130] With regard to family life, one key historical issue that local gravestone inscriptions help children to appreciate is the high levels of infant mortality that generally prevailed before the 20th century. The impact on families could be tragic, as the inscription below demonstrates.

In Memory Of
5 Children, Issue of JAMES and
SARAH EMERY, who died as follows.
MARY ANN, December 28th 1839
AGED 3 YEARS. 2nd MARY ANN Augt
9th, 1840 an Infant.
3rd MARY ANN, Decr 15th 1841 an
Infant. JOHN, October 17th, 1839
an Infant
SARAH ANN, September 7th 1847
an Infant.

127 T. Wiltshire, 'Telling and suggesting in the Conwy Valley', *Teaching History*, 100 (2000) pp.32-5.

128 H. Cooper, 'Churches as a local historical source', *Primary History*, 66 (2014), pp.32-3 and H. Cooper and P. Etchells, 'Church going – Kendal, *Teaching History*, 83 (1996), pp. 30-2.

129 K. Lindley, *Graves and Graveyards* (Routledge & Kegan Paul, 1972). For further details on these matters, see A. Bruce, *Monuments, Memorials and the Local Historian* (Historical Association, 1997).

130 B. Forrest, 'Stories in Stones: using cemeteries as a local history resource', *Primary History*, 69 (2015), pp.44-6.

The inscription, copied as it appears, is taken from a gravestone in St. Peter's churchyard, Preston. It shows that James and Sarah Emery lost five children, four of them infants. Parish register baptism entries record that James was a basket maker and that he and his wife had four other children, all girls. At least one of them, the fourth to be named Mary Ann, survived into adulthood. She was baptised in 1842 and in 1865, her child Clara Amelia was baptised, no father being named in the baptism register.

Unusual inscriptions on gravestones can have great appeal to both teacher and taught, especially when humour, sometimes uncomplimentary, is involved. Many examples are available online and in books. They include the legendary, and very economical, *Thorpe's corpse.*[131]

Using local war memorials as a starting point can also facilitate children's historical investigations, as Dale Banham and Chris Culpin have demonstrated. Taking as a theme the impact that World War I had at local level, they suggest several lines of enquiry that children can undertake. Counting the number of men who died in a locality and estimating the proportion they comprised of the young men there are examples. They note other insights into these men that can be gained by searching the Commonwealth War Graves Commission's web site, including the ranks they held and their age, date and place of death. From analysing this information, they note the type of questions that children can consider in assessing the nature and impact of World War I.[132] An exercise starting with World War I memorial details for Cottenham in Cambridgeshire has been reported by Geraint Brown and James Woodcock. Year 9 children were encouraged to ask questions about the men named on the memorial. Further details of these men were obtained from the *Roll of Honour* website maintained by the Ministry of Defence and the Royal British Legion. (The website is at <http://www.roll-of-honour.com/>.) A computer database was created, which the class used to explore definitions of historical significance.[133] Focusing on key stages 1 and 2, Ruth Cavender offers several teaching ideas relating to war memorials, including their design and the role they played in remembrance.[134]

131 Fritz Spiegl, *A Small Book of Graveyard Humour* (Pan, 1971) remains a classic of its type.

132 D. Banham with C. Culpin, 'Ensuring progression continues into GCSE: let's not do for our pupils with our plan of attack', *Teaching History*, 109 (December, 2002), pp.16-22. Ian Phillips has fed information from the same source into a computer database in order to assess the impact of World War I on local communities. See I. Phillips, 'Crime in Liverpool and First World War soldiers from Hull: using databases to explore the real depth in the data', *Teaching History*, 160 (September, 2015), pp.36-46.

133 G. Brown and J. Woodcock, 'Relevant, rigorous and revisited: using local history to make meaning of historical significance', *Teaching History*, 134 (March, 2009), pp.4-9.

134 R. Cavender, 'War memorials as a local history resource', *Primary History*, 67 (Summer, 2014), pp. 44-5.

Chapter 10

Local history teaching and potsherds

This chapter expands the comments made in chapters 3 and 4 about using artefacts in teaching local history. By so doing, evidence can be adduced to shed light on a variety of historical themes that children might investigate. However, the focus here is on how children can interpret the evidence that artefacts provide, thereby adding to their investigative skills. To this end, a start is made with an exercise that considers how they might make use of potsherds and other incomplete artefacts that can be found locally. The sections that follow address two other matters that arise in using artefacts as a teaching aid, irrespective of whether or not local history themes are being studied. One concerns the nature of the questions that children ask about the artefacts they use. The other deals with the ways in which exercises based on artefact investigation can be introduced in the classroom.

Observing potsherds

Potsherds tend to be small, though in some cases more than one piece relating to the same object can be found. Perhaps working in groups, children might handle a small collection of sherds, noting details about them.[135] Variety is important here, so that at least some of the sherds are from the edges of objects. Decorated and plain pieces might form part of the collection, as well as fragments from objects of different types. Tableware fragments are likely to predominate, but other items, such as pieces of clay pipe (stem or bowl) and school ink wells, might be included. The exercise might start by class discussion on how pottery is produced, so children are able to appreciate that it is made from clay heated to high temperatures in kilns; that it may be made in moulds or on a wheel; that decoration might be added to it by hand or transfer: and that glazes are applied to some or all of its surfaces, in part to make them moisture proof.[136]

The children could be asked to observe and make brief notes about the fragments. Alternatively, questions might be set to guide them. These could include some or all of the following, with or without clues:

- Do any of the pieces have decoration?
- Describe the decoration, including its colour or colours.
- Is the decoration on each side or just on one side?

---

135 Yosanna Vella notes the advice of teachers in the Avon area that the best way of using artefacts in the classroom with young children is through group work, so that each child has opportunity to study them. See Y. Vella, 'Artefacts in history education', *Primary History*, 54 (Spring, 2010), p.5. This issue of the journal is devoted to teaching and learning using objects.

136 Useful guidance can be found in D. Weldrake, *Steps in Identifying Pottery* at <http://www.archaeology.wyjs.org.uk/documents/archaeology/identifying/pottery.pdf>.

- How might the decoration have been put on?
- Do you like any of the decorations? Give a reason for your answer.
- Do any of the pieces fit together?
- Find any pieces that are from the edge of the object. (Clue: The edges will be glazed.)
- What do you think any of the items might be from? (Clue: Some of them are curved.)

The origins of the potsherds

A follow-up exercise takes children's understanding further by getting them to work out the diameters of the objects from which curved potsherds with edges probably came.[137] The aim in so doing is to shed light on what the objects were most likely to have been. The approach, as shown in the diagram below, is to create a circle for each of the potsherds that formed part of the edge of an object. The circumference of the circle must line up exactly with the external curve of the potsherd. In this way, the diameter of the object can be determined. Plainly, if the object is only a few centimetres in diameter it would not have been, say, a dinner plate. Equally, it would not have been an eggcup if its diameter was 30 centimetres.

The question arises as to how the circle might be created. To begin with, the potsherd is held upside down on a piece of paper, on which the line of the curve can then be drawn. Then, as the second diagram shows, the potsherd can be placed on part of the drawn line but extending beyond it. In this way, a larger amount of the object's circumference can be drawn. The process is repeated until the circumference is complete. A diameter measure can then be taken.

Another method is to use a pair of compasses. The third diagram shows the method involved. Again, the potsherd is held upside down on a piece of paper and the line of its curve is marked. A line AB – in effect a chord - is drawn from one end of the curve to the other. This line is bisected by another line CD running through it at right angles. To create this line, the centre point of AB is measured and marked. Line CD can then be drawn at right angles to AB, passing through its centre point. Since a pair of compasses is required for the exercise, the right angle can be created by drawing intersecting arcs from points A and B. The centre of the circle of which the curved line forms part lies along line CD. A little trial and error with the compasses will locate the centre point. The radius can then be determined and hence the diameter.

Children could draw the circles by either method. However, another approach could be tried using the resources shown below. As can be seen, four circles of differing sizes have been prepared for the children. Each circle is linked with one of the potsherds, thus showing its diameter. In the classroom, the potsherds, along with several others, are given to a group of children for preliminary observation, perhaps with some questions to address. The circles are then introduced, the children's task being to select the four potsherds that link with the circles. Having done so, they can try to determine the type of objects from which the potsherds came. The diameters will help them, along with other features the potsherds display.

137 The assumption is made that the curved potsherds were from round pieces of pottery, as opposed to square or oblong ones that had rounded corners. Children might consider this point.

Those shown in the illustration are from the bowl of a clay pipe (with nicotine staining); a dish; a dinner plate (with a serrated edge); and a school inkwell.

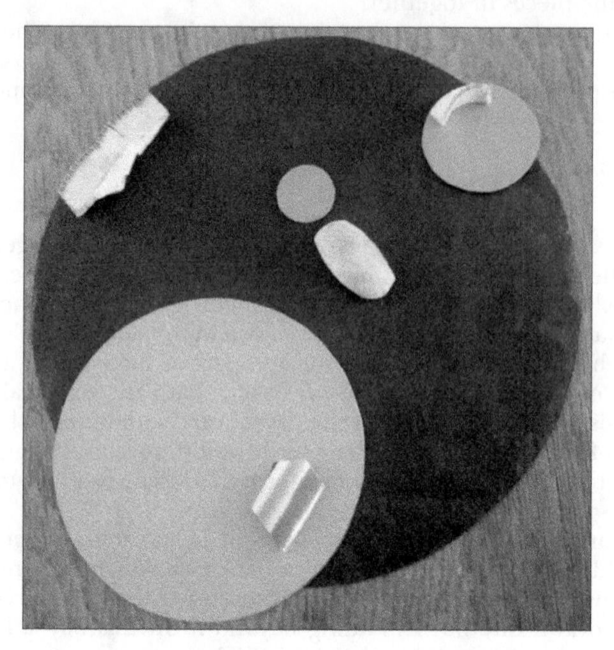

Potsherds and paper diameter circles.

Matters arising

Exercises based on potsherds and other sorts of incomplete artefacts help children to appreciate the difficulties that historians and archaeologists encounter in interpreting the evidence at their disposal. At the same time, these exercises demonstrate that evidence of this type can still have value in helping to determine the characteristics and usage of the artefacts that past generations created. They also show that even small fragments of artefacts can prove revealing in these respects.

The potsherd exercise also has use value in enabling children to engage with aspects of circle geometry. The terminology involved is one matter. Another is the appreciation that the diameter of a circle is twice its radius. Should children be aware of this relationship, they will have occasion to apply it. However, the exercise can be undertaken without this knowledge.[138]

It may be that working with fragments of artefacts rather than complete ones can be seen as more challenging for children. If so, a means of achieving progression is to hand. Yet using whole objects in relation to specific themes that children investigate, whether at a local or more general level, can also enable them to gain valuable insights, as well as giving them opportunity to apply and deepen their understanding. Scrutiny of the much-revered flat iron, for example, can have high

138 A detailed discussion of how teenage children tackled an exercise of this type can be found on the website of Drexel University, Philadelphia at <http://mathforum.org/pow/teacher/samples/MathForumSampleGeometryPacket.pdf>.

use value as one piece of evidence that children can use in investigating the hard labour involved in running a non-mechanised home.[139]

David Wright has written about the way in which seven-year olds at Mulbarton First School in Norfolk discovered and collected their own potsherds and the classification they made of the different types. He notes the conclusions they drew and gives an alternative classification of the children's finds made by a museum teacher.[140] The potsherds they used could not be dated with any precision, though perhaps some may have reached back into the Victorian era. With regard to the more distant past, Ian Wibberley has reported how a selection of Roman artefact fragments collected and documented in the Enfield area by the local archaeological society were made into five sets of artefacts for classroom use. Sheets of background notes and other teaching aids were also prepared.[141]

Questioning artefacts

Several of the questions relating to potsherds given at the start of this chapter deal with their appearance and are intended to elicit factual responses. They are useful in inviting children to make close observations about the nature of the potsherds. They may also help to awaken interest and, since the questions are simple, to give confidence in responding.

More demanding questions are also included. That concerning the objects of which the potsherds might be a part is an example. Essentially, children are being asked to make reasoned responses based on the evidence they have to hand. This evidence is insufficient to enable them to draw firm conclusions, though they are given guidance by being alerted to the fact that some of the potsherds are curved. Also more demanding is the question about whether or not they like any of the decoration on the potsherds. This question could take them beyond historical considerations, though it might also lead to discussion on changes in taste that have occurred over time in the design and appearance of objects.

One issue that emerges from these observations is that of how much direction children should be given from questions set by teachers when making use of the evidence that artefacts provide. It is noted in chapter 4 that concern has been expressed, at least with regard to key stage 1, that too much teacher intervention might stifle children's imagination, whereas leaving the questioning largely, if not solely, to them might give rise to more interesting and challenging activities. On the other hand, insufficient guidance might lead to missed opportunities in achieving historical understanding. The approach suggested by Scott Harrison and Richard Woff helps to overcome this problem. They require children to make individual written comments on an object they view as a prelude to class discussion in which fact and opinion feature. In the light of this discussion, and of additional information provided by the teacher, groups of children can make and compare their interpretations of the object.[142] In describing artefact-based work that they

---

139 See Appendix 1 for further details.

140 D. Wright, 'A small local investigation', *Teaching History*, 39 (June, 1984), pp.3-4.

141 I. Wibberley, 'Developing local history materials in Enfield', *Teaching History*, 39 (June, 1984), pp.21-3.

142 S. Harrison and R. Woff, 'Using museums and artefacts', *Primary History*, 37 (Summer,

undertook with primary school children of varying ages, Liz Smith and Cathy Holden stress the importance of the teacher's role in 'endorsing and clarifying children's hypotheses and scaffolding their learning'.[143]

What is important in using objects, however, is for children to ask the type of questions that transcend simple observation. Being content only to describe the features of objects enables them to make limited use of the evidence that the objects provide. Also, they avoid grappling with the uncertainties that arise when more demanding questions are set. A progression issue presents itself here, with more sophisticated questioning of objects being expected as children proceed through the key stages. And it may be in this context that teacher intervention has an appreciable role to play.

Introducing artefacts in the classroom

Various suggestions can be found in the literature concerning ways in which artefact exercises can be introduced in the classroom with the aim of stimulating children's curiosity. The following, all of which are valuable in teaching local history, are examples.

Displaying objects

Helen Horler advocates a straightforward approach, arguing that placing a collection of artefacts in the middle of a table is sufficient to engage children's interest, since the basic instinct of 'wanting to touch' is aroused.[144] The Nuffield Primary History Project also suggests displaying objects, but by dispersing them around the classroom on desks covered in sugar paper. This 'object carousel' approach enables groups of children to spend five minutes with each object recording their observations and questions on the sugar paper.[145]

Objects in containers

Yosanne Vella relates how the artefacts she used were hidden in a large plastic box. They were then shown one at a time to the children, who waited excitedly for each one to appear.[146] With Grant Bage's 'lucky dip' approach, a child withdraws one of the artefacts from a box or bag and has to describe it to the others, who are blindfolded or have their backs turned. The child is not allowed to state what the object is and the audience have to find out from the description given.[147]

2004), pp.18-20.

143 L. Smith and C. Holden, 'I thought it was for picking bones out of soup ... using artefacts in the primary school', *Teaching History*, 76 (June, 1994), pp.6-9.

144 H. Horler, 'Artefact handling at Brunel's SS Great Britain ... touch, look, listen, smell – but please don't taste', *Primary History*, 54 (Spring, 2010), p.28.

145 Details can be found at <https://www.history.org.uk/primary/module/ 3657/primary-teaching-methods>.

146 Y. Vella, 'Extending primary children's thinking through the use of artefacts', *Primary History*, 54 (Spring, 2010), p.15.

147 G. Bage, 'History, artefacts and storytelling in the 2011 primary curriculum', *Primary History*, 54 (Spring, 2010), p.24.

Covering objects

For an exercise dealing with a Year 1 project on homes and houses in the past, Claire Eley describes how she wrapped up several Victorian artefacts individually. They included a kettle, a flat iron and a washboard. Her class worked in groups and each group was given one of the covered objects, which they handled. Comments they made were noted and read back to them before they were asked to guess what the objects were. The children were reminded of their comments and guesses before being allowed to unwrap the objects.[148] John Davis relates how he wrapped the artefacts he used with his class of ten- and eleven-year olds, observing not only that the unwrapping had to be undertaken carefully, but also that instant decisions had to be made about how the objects should be held.[149] Last but not least, John Fines reports how he posted objects to school that were wrapped in many layers of paper. The packages were tied tightly and sealing wax was applied. He reasoned that the harder it is to get at an object, the more special it seems. He also placed objects in an old tin box, which was difficult to open using a wonky key, and hid small objects in his hand or pocket.[150]

Conclusion

Artefacts can play a valuable part in children's local history investigations, adding to the evidence they can glean from other types of source. They have particular value as far as younger children are concerned, but they can be used to telling effect by all age groups. Emphasis seems to be on using whole objects rather than parts of objects, but both can be used to generate children's interest, with a variety of enterprising approaches having been suggested. And both can be used to challenge them to make reasoned interpretations arising from close observation and questioning, which can extend beyond matters of usage to those of design characteristics.

148 *Houses: Artefacts for the past* forms part of the Nuffield Primary History Project resources. Further details can be found at <http://www.history.org.uk/resources/primary_resources_136.html>.

149 J. Davis, 'Artefacts in the primary school', *Teaching History*, 45 (June, 1986), pp.6-8.

150 J. Fines, '"Doing history" with objects', *Primary History*, 54 (Spring, 2010), p.7.

Conclusion

Including local history in the primary and secondary school curriculum makes considerable demands on teachers. A great deal of thought and effort is needed in planning the provision they make, not least in devising appropriate learning activities. The absence of local history textbooks creates the need to generate learning resources that children of differing ages and abilities can use effectively. Moreover, since heavy reliance has to be made on primary evidence, issues of selection and adaptation for classroom use have to be carefully considered.

Fortunately, help is at hand. Throughout the country, a varied range of primary source material can be readily accessed and copied at minimal cost. Local libraries, museums, record offices and art galleries have a key role to play in making this material available for classroom use, but other organisations, including local history and archaeological societies may also be able to make important contributions, as may local colleges and universities. Increasingly, too, local history sources are becoming available online and, albeit at some cost, in compact disc form. Furthermore, the local built environment and the reminiscences of local people add greatly to the range of evidence available.

Offering additional help are practitioners' reports about the ways in which local history teaching has been undertaken in primary and secondary schools. Quite a number of these reports are mentioned in this guide, though, for the most part, the selection made has been limited to those dealing with themes covered in the exercise chapters. Even so, a substantial literature is available that reports inspired and successful classroom approaches in teaching local history, involving children in varied types of investigative activity. Perhaps, in relating this activity, more might have emerged at times about contextualisation and the historical understanding that children attained, particularly beyond key stage 1. And the same point might be made with regard to some of the suggested activities that receive mention. Recourse to the secondary literature can certainly help in addressing these matters. Yet reflective practice clearly prevails, with clear objectives being stated, attention being drawn to issues encountered and comment being made on possible improvements. Stimulating contributions are certainly being made to the scholarship of learning and teaching.

What is also evident from the literature is that, as is appropriate, children at each key stage are being presented with challenging activities in their local history investigations. They not only have to become familiar with different types of historical sources, but also to extract and interpret evidence contained in the sources that is relevant to the task in hand. They are also encouraged to ask questions that facilitate their investigations; to evaluate the reliability of the evidence; to work in groups; and to articulate and present their findings in varying formats. In other words, they are given opportunity to develop the types of key skills on which high value is placed by modern educationalists and which are also prized in the world of work, as well as in everyday life.

The final word can be left to the children by drawing on the telling reactions made to a course on local history taught by John Mathews in a Bristol school during the early 1980s.[151] The children used several types of primary sources in the work they undertook and 81 of them responded to questions about it. Of these sources, the most popular proved to be transcriptions of 1851 census enumerators' schedules relating to four local villages. They were voted in first position by 25 children, approaching a third of them. Next most popular were school log book extracts, which received the votes of 19 children, almost a quarter. These two sources were far ahead of any others, with a tithe map and schedule, which attracted ten votes, leading the trailing pack, amongst which was trade directory and parish register evidence. Other results from the survey were that sizeable majorities of children preferred their studies of local history to those of American history and the use of primary evidence rather than of textbooks or a mixture of both. These results are stated with due qualification, but they do suggest that teaching investigative local history has strong appeal as far as children are concerned.

151 J. Mathews, 'A course of local history for 11-12 year olds and their reaction to it', *Teaching History*, 34 (October, 1982), pp.7-12.

Appendix 1
Contemporary illustrations of household artefacts

Box irons

The box irons shown here contained a metal heater (known as a slug) that could be removed and re-heated in the kitchen fire or on the kitchen range as need arose. Two slugs would be provided so that one could be heating whilst the other was in use. The slug, made from cast iron, was loaded by opening the top of the iron and was held in the base of the iron by a locating pin. The top was secured to the base with a fastening device operated by a lever. (The alternative was to insert the slug through a vertically-sliding door at the back of the iron.) Care was clearly needed when inserting the slug. For safety reasons, a wooden handle with a metal hand shield beneath was provided. A box iron had advantage over a flat iron in that it did not need to be placed close to the heat source. The risk of soot falling on the bottom of the iron was countered, therefore. The examples shown here were made by the West Bromwich firm of Joseph and Jesse Siddons.

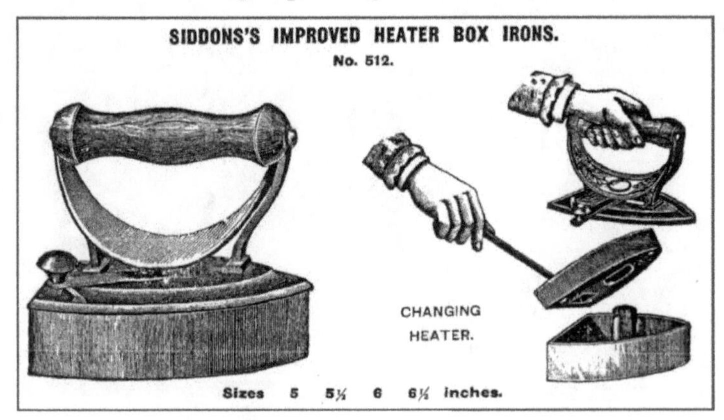

Source: *Peck's Circular Trades Directory* (Birmingham, 1896-7), p.34. This directory can be seen at <http://specialcollections.le.ac.uk/cdm/landingpage/collection/p16445coll4>.

Chamber candlesticks

Candlesticks of this type were designed to be carried around the house. They comprised a short stem and a carrying handle set in a drip pan. In the examples shown, a Randell's patent handle was also fitted to the top of each stem. This device comprised short, spring-loaded handles and curved jaws that were linked by a pivot. (Comparison can be made with a pair of pliers.) Squeezing the handles together opened the jaws, allowing them to grip the candle. The handles could then be released, leaving the candle held firmly in position. Apart from providing a safety feature, the device brought advantage because, as the illustration shows, candles of differing diameter could be held in the stem.

Source: *Peck's Circular Trades Directory* (Birmingham, 1896-7), p.341.

Bibliography

Contextual sources

1. Books and articles

J. P. Allen, *Practical Building Construction* (Crosby Lockwood, 1900).
A. Bruce, *Monuments, Memorials and the Local Historian* (Historical Association, 1997).
R. W. Brunskill, *Traditional Buildings of Britain: An Introduction to Vernacular Architecture and Its Revival* (Cassell, third edition, 2004).
R. W. Brunskill and A. Clifton-Taylor, *English Brickwork* (Ward Lock, 1977).
J. Burnett, *A Social History of Housing, 1815-1970* (Methuen, 1978).
P. Carter and K. Thompson, *Sources for Local Historians* (Phillimore, 2005).
C. D. Cragoe, *How To Read Buildings: A Crash Course in Architecture* (Bloomsbury Publishing, 2008).
J. E. Crowther and P. A. Crowther, *The Diary of Robert Sharp of South Cave: Life in a Yorkshire Village, 1812-1837* (Oxford University Press, 1997).
S. J. Curtis, *History of Education in Great Britain* (University Tutorial Press 1961 reprint).
D. Defoe, *A Tour Through the Whole Island of Great Britain* (1986 reprint of 1724-6 edition).
E. Gadd, *Victorian Logs* (Brewin, 1979).
P. Gordon and D. Lawton, *Curriculum Change in the Nineteenth and Twentieth Centuries* (Hodder & Stoughton, 1978).
P. Hanks, K. Hardcastle and F. Hodges, *A Dictionary of First Names* (Oxford University Press, second edition, 2006).
J. B. Harley, *Maps for the Local Historian* (The Standing Conference for Local History, 1977).
E. Higgs, *Making Sense of the Census Revisited: Census Records for England and Wales, 1801-1901* (Institute of Historical Research, 2005).
B. P. Hindle, *Maps for Local History* (Batsford, 1988).
Home and Colonial School Society, *A Manual of Elementary Instruction* (fifth edition, 1884).
W. G. Hoskins, *The Making of the English Landscape* (Penguin reprint, 1973).
K. Lindley, *Graves and Graveyards* (Routledge & Kegan Paul, 1972).
S. T. Miller, 'The value of photographs as historical evidence', *The Local Historian*, 15 (1983), pp.468-73.
S. Muthesius, *The English Terraced House* (Yale University Press, 1982).
J. L. Notter and R. H. Firth, *Hygiene* (Longmans,1894).
R. Oliver, *Ordnance Survey Maps: A Concise Guide for Historians* (The Charles Close Society, 1993).
G. Oliver, *Photographs and Local History* (Batsford,1989).
G. Redmonds, *Christian Names in Local and Family History* (Dundurn, 2004).
P. Riden, *Local History: A Handbook for Beginners* (Batsford, 1983).
E. E. Robson, *School Architecture* (Leicester University Press, 1972 reprint of 1874

edition).
R. Rodger, *Housing in Urban Britain, 1780-1914* (MacMillan, 1989).
G. Shaw and A. Tipper, *British Directories* (Mansell, second edition, 1997).
S. Smith-Bannister, *Names and Naming Patterns in England, 1538-1750* (Oxford University Press, 1997).
F. Spiegl, *A Small Book of Graveyard Humour* (Pan, 1971).
W. B. Stephens, *Sources for English Local History* (Manchester University Press, 1973).
M. Sturt, *The Education of the People* (Routledge & Kegan Paul, 1967).
K. Tiller, *English Local History: An Introduction* (Sutton, 2002).
S. Wood, 'Social history from school log books', *The Local Historian*, 14 (1981), pp.471-6.

2. *Websites*

A History of Migration at <http://www.geography.org.uk/search.asp?searchfor=migration& searchin=all>.
B. H. Babbage, *Report to the General Board of Health on … Haworth* (HMSO, 1850) extracts at <https://www.bl.uk/collection-items/sanitary-report-on-haworth-home-to-the-bronts>.
BBC *A Guide to Oral History* at <http://downloads.bbc.co.uk/history/handsonhistory/ a_guide_to_oral_history.pdf>.
BBC *Local History Trails* at <http://www.bbc.co.uk/history/trail/local_history/>.
BBC *Legacies* at <http://www.bbc.co.uk/legacies/>.
BBC *Millennium Memory Bank* at <http://sounds.bl.uk/Accents-and-dialects/Millenium-memory-bank>.
BBC *WW2 People's War* at <http://www.bbc.co.uk/ww2peopleswar/>.
Behind the Name at <http://www.behindthename.com/top/>.
Britain From Above at <http://www.britainfromabove.org.uk/>.
British Association for Local History at <http://www.balh.org.uk/>.
British Film Institute, Britain on Film at <http://player.bfi.org.uk/britain-on-film/>.
Court Leet Records (Preston, Manchester, Salford and Southampton) at <https://archive.org/ search.php?query=court%20leet%20records>.
East Anglian Film Archive at <http://www.eafa.org.uk/>.
East Midlands Oral History Archive at <https://www.le.ac.uk/emoha/>.
East Riding Archive Maps at <http://treasurehouse.eastriding.gov.uk/Help.aspx>.
Education in England: the history of our schools at <http://www.educationengland.org.uk/history/ index.html>.
From Weaver to Web at <http://www.calderdale.gov.uk/wtw/>.
D. A. Galbi, *Long-Term Trends in Personal Given Name Frequencies in the UK* (2002) at <http://www.galbithink.org/names.htm>.
Sir George Head, *A Home Tour Through the Manufacturing Districts of England during the Summer of 1835* (Cass 1968 reprint of the 1836 edition) at <https://babel.hathitrust.org/cgi/ pt?id=uc2.ark:/13960/t9z03b223;view=1up;seq=5http://catalog.hathitrust.org/Record/001315340>.
Historical Association at <https://www.history.org.uk/>.
Historical Directories of England and Wales at http://www.historicaldirectories.org/hd/index.asp>.
Historic England Heritage Explorer at <http://www.heritageexplorer.org.uk>.
History House (mainly Essex sources) at <http://www.historyhouse.co.uk/index.html>.
Joined Up Heritage Sheffield: Local History at < https://www.

joinedupheritagesheffield.org.uk/content/ resources/local-history>.
Local Suffragettes at <http://localsuffragettes.wikispaces.com/>.
London's Pulse: Medical Officer of Health Reports, 1848-1972 at <http://wellcomelibrary.org/moh/>.
Looking at Buildings at <http://www.lookingatbuildings.org.uk/index.html>.
Maps of Lancashire at <http://www3.lancashire.gov.uk/environment/oldmap/>.
Mingulay and St. Kilda school log books at <http://www.nas.gov.uk/about/110908.asp>.
My Learning at <http://www.mylearning.org/>.
National Library of Scotland Map Images at <http://maps.nls.uk/index.html>.
Newman University Local History at <http://www.newmanlocalhistory.org.uk/>.
'Night soil and other euphemisms', *Parks and Gardens UK* at <https://parksandgardensuk.wordpress.com/2015/07/11/night-soil-and-other-euphemisms/>.
Norfolk Record Office Information Leaflet 45: Parish Registers at <http://www.archives.norfolk. gov.uk/view/NCC098531>.
North West Film Archive at <https://www.nwfa.mmu.ac.uk/>.
Office for National Statistics, *Immigration Patterns of Non-UK Born Populations in England and Wales in 2011* (December, 2013) at <http://www.ons.gov.uk/ons/dcp171776_346219.pdf>.
Office for National Statistics, *Neighbourhood Statistics* at <http://www.neighbourhood.statistics. gov.uk/dissemination/>.
Online Parish Clerks Project at <http://onlineparishclerks.org.uk/>.
Oxford University's Migration Observatory at <http://www. migrationobservatory.ox.ac.uk/ projects/migration-in-the-census>.
Pitwork at <http://www.dmm.org.uk/pitwork/html/daz.htm>.
Primary Sources (North East England) at <http://www.primarysources.org.uk/about.php>.
Richard Heaton's Newspaper at <http://freepages.genealogy.rootsweb.ancestry.com/~dutillieul/ ZOtherPapers/Index.html>.
Roll of Honour at <http://www.roll-of-honour.com/Derbyshire/index.html>.
Scottish Screen Archive at <http://ssa.nls.uk/>.
Society of Genealogists, *Guide 3: Census Records (England and Wales)* at <http://www.sog.org.uk/ learn/help-getting-started-with-genealogy/guide-four/>.
Somerset Voices Oral History Archive at <http://www.somersetvoices.org.uk/>.
The Big Smoke: London on Film at <www.youtube.com/playlist?list=PL2189B4FCA011C2A1>.
The Coalmining History Resource Centre at <https://archive.is/www.cmhrc.co.uk>.
The Condition and Treatment of the Children Employed in the Mines and Collieries of the United Kingdom (Strange, 1842) at <http://www.bl.uk/collection-items/report-on-child-labour-1842>.
The copper (set pot) water heater at <http://www.1900s.org.uk/copper-water-heater.htm>.
The National Archives Education at <http://www.nationalarchives.gov.uk/education/>.
G. Timmins, *Working Life and The First Modern Census* at <http://www.bbc.co.uk/history/trail/ victorian_britain/earning_a_living/working_life_census_01.shtml>.
Valley of Stone at <http://www.valleyofstone.org.uk/journey/stoneinthelandscape/fashions>.
Victoria County History at <http://www.victoriacountyhistory.ac.uk/about>.
T. Wainwright (ed.), *Barnstaple Parish Register, 1538-1812* (Commin, 1903) at

<https://archive.org/ stream/registerofbaptisoobyubarn#page/n7/ mode/2up>.

A. S. Welch, *Object Lessons: Prepared for Teachers of Primary Schools and Primary Classes* (Barnes, 1862) at <https://archive.org/details/objectlessonspreoowelcrich>.

D. Weldrake, *Steps in Identifying Pottery* at <http://www. archaeology.wyjs.org.uk/ documents/ archaeology/identifying/pottery.pdf>.

West Sussex County Council Learning Resources at <http://www.westsussex.gov.uk/ learning/learning_resources.aspx>.

Yorkshire Film Archive at <http://www.yorkshirefilmarchive.com/>.

A. Young, *A Six Weeks Tour through the Southern Counties of England and Wales* (1769) at <https://archive.org/details/asixweekstourthooyougoog>.

Learning and teaching sources

1. Books and articles

L. Abbot and R. S. Grayson, 'Community engagement in local history: a report on the Hemel at War project', *Teaching History*, 145 (December, 2012), pp.4-12.

R. Alfano, 'Databases, spreadsheets and historical enquiry at key stage 3', *Teaching History*, 101 (November, 2000), pp.42-7.

M. Anderson, 'Oral history: a source of evidence for children in the primary classroom', *Primary History*, 55 (Summer, 2010), pp.32-3.

G. Bage, 'History, artefacts and storytelling in the 2011 primary curriculum', *Primary History*, 54 (Spring, 2010), pp.23-4.

D. Banham with C. Culpin, 'Ensuring progression continues into GCSE: let's not do for our pupils with our plan of attack', *Teaching History*, 109 (December, 2002), pp.16-22.

J. Barkham, 'Local history and literacy using written (and other) sources', *Primary History*, 64 (Summer, 2013), pp.28-9.

P. Barrett, '"My grandfather slammed the door in Winston Churchill's face!": using family history to provoke rigorous enquiry', *Teaching History*, 145 (December, 2011), pp.14-21.

K. C. Barton, 'Helping students make sense of historical time', *Primary History*, 37 (Summer, 2004), pp.13-14.

A. Blyth, *et.al.*, *Place, Time and Society 8-13: Curriculum Planning in History, Geography and Social Science* (Collins, 1976).

J. Blyth, *History in Primary Schools* (Open University Press, 1989).

G. Brown and J. Woodcock, 'Relevant, rigorous and revisited: using local history to make meaning of historical significance', *Teaching History*, 134 (March, 2009), pp.4-11.

J. Card, 'Talking pictures: exploiting the potential of visual sources to generate productive pupil talk', *Teaching History*, 148 (September, 2012), pp.40-6.

A. Carter, 'What your local archive service can offer to schools', *Primary History*, 70 (June, 2015), pp.40-1.

N. Caskey, 'A project on working-class education in the Victorian period', *Primary History*, 36 (Spring, 2004), pp.24-6.

S. Catling, 'Geography and history: exploring the local connection', *Primary History*, 42 (Spring, 2006), pp.14-6.

R. Cavender, 'War memorials as a local history resource', *Primary History*, 67 (Summer, 2014), pp. 44-5.

H. Claire, 'Oral History: a powerful tool or a double-edged sword?', *Primary History*,

38 (Winter, 2004), pp.20-3.
H. Claire, 'Planning for diversity in the key stage 2 history curriculum: the Victorians', *Primary History*, 28 (May, 2001), pp.6-9.
G. Clemitshaw, 'Have we got the question right? Engaging future citizens in local history enquiry', *Teaching History*, 106 (March, 2002), pp.20-7.
H. Cooper, 'Churches as a local historical source', *Primary History*, 66 (2014), pp.32-3.
H. Cooper, *The Teaching of History in Primary Schools* (David Fulton Publishers, third edition, 2000).
H. Cooper and P. Etchells, 'Church going – Kendal,' *Teaching History*, 83 (1996), pp.30-2.
M. Corbishley, 'Our heritage: use it or lose it', *Primary History*, 51 (Spring, 2008), pp.8-9.
E. M. Corrigan, 'Battling on: family history in the primary classroom', *Teaching History*, 81 (October, 1995), pp.14-18.
R. Coulthard and R. Patterson, 'History through streets', *Primary History*, 12, (November, 1996), pp.6-8.
I. Cramer, 'Oral history: working with children', *Teaching History*, 71 (April, 1993), pp.11-19.
J. Davis, 'Artefacts in the primary school', *Teaching History*, 45 (June, 1986), pp.6-8.
L. M. Davies and J. A. H. Evans, 'Tales from the ironworks in Blaenavon: the Industrial Revolution and the Children's Employment Act of 1842', *Primary History*, 31 (Spring, 2002), pp.31-6.
J. Dean, 'Nuffield Primary History and classroom archaeology', *Primary History*, 51 (Spring, 2009), pp.14-15.
J. Dean, 'The power of the visual image in learning: the Nuffield Primary History approach', *Primary History*, 49 (Summer, 2008), pp.22-3.
L. Dixon and A. Hales, *Bringing History Alive Through Local People and Places* (Routledge, 2014).
F. Dodwell, 'The Jill Grey collection and Hitchin British schools', *Primary History*, 27 (January 2001), pp.19-24.
I. Doncaster, *Finding the History Around Us* (Blackwell, 1957).
C. Edwards, 'Putting life into history: how pupils can use oral history to become critical historians', *Teaching History*, 123 (June, 2006), pp.21-5.
D. Evans, 'A small oral history project in four rural Cumbrian primary schools', *Teaching History*, 57 (October, 1989), pp.25-7.
J. Fines, '"Doing history" with objects', *Primary History*, 54 (Spring, 2010), pp.6-7.
J. Fines, 'Doing local history', *Primary History*, 55 (Summer, 2010), pp.6-7.
M. Fogg, 'The use of sixteenth/seventeenth century wills and inventories as historical sources in the primary school', *Teaching History*, 80 (June, 1995), pp.27-30.
A. Ford, 'Setting us free? Building meaningful models of progression for a "post-levels" world', *Teaching History*, 157 (December, 2014), pp.28-41.
B. Forrest, 'Stories in Stones: using cemeteries as a local history resource', *Primary History*, 69 (2015), pp.44-5.
General National Curriculum Council, *History Non-Statutory Guidance* (NNC, 1991).
H. Glendinning and G. Timmins, 'Population history with juniors: using parish registers', *Teaching History*, 36 (June, 1983), pp.16-18.
G. Guest, 'Looking at buildings as a source for developing historical enquiries', *Primary History*, 28 (May, 2001), pp.15-17.
J. Halewood, 'A treasure trove of local history – how to use your local record office', *Primary*

J. Halewood, 'Using school log books – Bishop Graham Memorial Ragged School, Chester', *Primary History*, 24 (January, 2000), pp.22-4.
P. Hammond, 'A load of rubbish: using Victorian throwaways in the classroom', *Primary History*, 36 (Spring, 2004), pp.12-15.
K. Hann, 'Migration: the search for a better life', *Primary History*, 37 (Summer, 2004), pp.6-9.
History, 24 (January, 2000), pp.10-11.
P. Harnett, 'Foundation stage and key stage 1 history [early years]: history and citizenship education – teaching sensitive issues, part 1', *Primary History*, 45 (Spring, 2007), pp.31-3.
P. Harnett and S. Whitehouse, 'Creative exploration of local, national and global links' in H. Cooper (ed), *Teaching History Creatively* (Routledge, 2013).
S. Harrison and R. Woff, 'Using museums and artefacts', *Primary History*, 37 (Summer, 2004), pp.18-20.
A. Hellon and E. Amis-Hughes, 'My learning: bringing history to life', *Primary History*, 61 (Summer, 2012), pp.17-19.
A. Hodkinson, 'Enhancing temporal cognition, practical activities for the primary classroom', *Primary History*, 28 (May, 2001), pp.11-14.
A. Hodkinson, 'Using the visual image in primary schools: a beginners' guide', *Primary History*, 49 (Summer, 2008), pp.14-15.
P. Hoodless, 'A Victorian case study: simulating aspects of Victorian life in the classroom', *Primary History*, 7 (June, 1994), pp.14-16.
P. Hoodless, *Teaching History in Primary Schools* (Sage, 2008).
H. Horler, 'Artefact handling at Brunel's SS Great Britain ... touch, look, listen, smell – but please don't taste', *Primary History*, 54 (Spring, 2010), pp.27-30.
A. Hughes and H. De Silva, 'One Street, twenty children and the experience of a changing town: year 7 explore the story of a London street', *Teaching History*, 151 (June, 2013), pp.55-63.
M. Johansen and M. Spafford, '"How our area used to be back then: an oral history project in an east London school', *Teaching History*, 134 (March, 2009), pp.37-46.
S. Kirkland, 'Learning about the past through "ourselves and our families"', *Primary History*, 75 (Spring, 2017), pp.6-7.
D. Knapp, 'A good place for an investigation: using sources to develop a local history project', *Primary History*, 16 (June, 1997), pp.4-6.
P. Knight, *History at Key Stages 1 & 2* (Longman, 1991).
R. Knights, 'Developing a local history project based on a local industry', *Primary History*, 39 (Spring, 2005), pp.32-3.
S. Leach, 'Teaching about my school in the past using original sources or why would I want those old books in my classroom?', *Primary History*, 73 (Summer, 2016), pp.22-5.
T. Lomas, 'A Local history investigation at key stage 2', *Primary History*, 75 (Spring 2017), pp.22-6.
T. Lomas, 'History co-ordinators' dilemma: pedagogy and the visual image', *Primary History*, 49 (Summer, 2008), pp.10-11.
T. Lomas, 'How do we ensure really good local history in primary schools?', *Primary History*, 30 (January, 2002), pp.4-6.
T. Lomas (ed.), 'Some teaching and learning strategies: planning and teaching local history', *Primary History*, 25 (June, 2000), pp.14-19.
J. Mathews, 'A course of local history for 11-12 year olds and their reaction to it', *Teaching History*, 34 (October, 1982), pp.7-9.
R. McFahn, S. Herrity and N. Bates, 'Riots, railways and Hampshire hill fort:

exploiting local history for rigorous evidential enquiry', *Teaching History*, 134 (March, 2009), pp.16-23.
M. Mills, 'Accessing archive sources', *Primary History*, 34 (May, 2003), pp.24-6.
M. Mills, 'Turn your pupils into history detectives: using sources to interpret old photographs', *Primary History*, 38 (Winter, 2004), pp.34-5.
National Curriculum Council, 'Non-statutory guidance for history', Department of Education and Science, *History in the National Curriculum (England)*, HMSO, 1991.
National Curriculum History Working Party, *Interim Report* (Department of Education and Science and the Welsh Office, 1989).
R. Noall, 'How can the use of spreadsheets enhance children's learning in history: a case study', *Primary History*, 26 (October, 2000), pp.16-17.
Nuffield Primary History Project, 'Local history field work – top ten pointers for success', *Primary History*, 55 (Summer, 2010), p.15.
J. Ould-Okojie, 'Exploring our roots: oral history in the local community', *Primary History*, 46 (Summer, 2007), pp.18-19.
M. Parsons, 'Asking the right questions: a study of the ability of KS 2 children to devise and use questions as part of their own research', *Primary History*, 26 (October, 2000), pp.12-13.
M. L. Parsons, 'Let's grab a granny off the street: the problems of oral history and how they can be minimalised', *Teaching History*, 84 (June, 1996), pp.30-3.
I. Phillips, 'Crime in Liverpool and First World War soldiers from Hull: using databases to explore the real depth in the data', *Teaching History*, 160 (September, 2015), pp.36-46.
I. Phillips, 'History and mathematics or history with mathematics: does it add up?', *Teaching History*, 107 (June, 2002), pp.35-40.
T. Pickford, 'On the canal', *Primary History*, 5 (November, 1993), pp.9-11.
H. Pluckrose, *Children Learning History* (Blackwell, 1991).
S. Purkis, *A Teacher's Guide to Using School Buildings* (English Heritage, 1993).
S. Purkis, *Oral History in Schools* (Oral History Society, no date).
A Redfern, 'Oral history in primary schools', *Primary History*, 23 (October,1999), pp.14-16.
A. Redfern, *Taking in Class: Oral History and the National Curriculum* (Oral History Society, 1996).
J. W. Robertson, '"No one else knows this": Scottish primary schools using ICT to investigate local history', *Primary History*, 29 (October, 2001), pp.7-9.
G. Rogers, 'The use of primary evidence in the junior school classroom', *Teaching History*, 38 (February, 1984), pp.22-5.
P. Rogers, '"Silver linings": using the elderly as a resource', *Primary History*, 10 (June, 1995), pp.14-15.
M. Rose, 'What the Dickens? Some views of the Victorians', *Primary History*, 34 (2003), pp.17-21.
Schools Council History 13-16 Project, *History Around Us: Some Guidelines for Teachers* (Holmes McDougall, 1976).
D. Smart, '"Balloons over Barton Hill": recreating the Bristol Blitz using artefacts and role play', *Primary History*, 31 (Spring, 2002), pp.18-21.
L. Smith and C. Holden, 'I thought it was for picking bones out of soup ... using artefacts in the primary school', *Teaching History*, 76 (June, 1994), pp.6-9.
M. Spafford, 'Thinking about local history', *Teaching History*, 149 (December, 2012), pp.4-7.
D. J. Steel and L. Taylor, *Family History in Schools* (Phillimore, 1973).
W. B. Stephens, *Teaching Local History* (Manchester University Press, 1977).

T. Sudell, 'Let's adopt a monument: a school's approach to covering history, literacy, science, and citizenship in an interesting way', *Primary History*, 22 (April, 1999), pp.18-21.
R. Unwin, *The Visual Dimension in the Study and Teaching of History* (Historical Association Teaching History Series, 49, 1981).
Y. Vella, 'Artefacts in history education', *Primary History*, 54 (Spring, 2010), p.5.
Y. Vella, 'Extending primary children's thinking through the use of artefacts', *Primary History*, 54 (Spring, 2010), p.14-17.
J. Watson and P. Harnett, 'What was it like when you were at school?', *Primary History*, 15 (February,1997), pp.10-12.
D. Welbourne, 'Deconstruction to reconstruction: an approach to women's history through local history', *Teaching History*, 59 (April, 1990), pp.16-22.
I. Wibberley, 'Developing local history materials in Enfield', *Teaching History*, 39 (June, 1984), pp.21-3.
T. Wiltshire, 'Telling and suggesting in the Conwy Valley', *Teaching History*, 100 (2000), pp.32-5.
D. Wright, 'A small local investigation', *Teaching History*, 39 (June, 1984), pp.3-4.

2. Learning and teaching websites

About Nuffield Primary History at <https://www.history.org.uk/primary/resource/3979/about-nuffield-primary-history>.
Department for Education, *History GCSE Subject Content* (April, 2014) at <https://www.gov.uk/ government/publications/gcse-history>.
Look Again! at <http://old.bfi.org.uk/education/teaching/lookagain/>.
National Curriculum for England at <https://www.gov.uk/government/collections/national-curriculum>.
Nuffield Primary History at <http://www.nuffieldfoundation.org/nuffield-primaryhistory-0>.
Nuffield Primary History: Teaching Methods at <https://www.history.org.uk/primary/module/ 3657/ primary-teaching-methods>.
Schools History Project at <http://www.schoolshistoryproject.org.uk/index.php>.
The Math Forum: Broken Pottery at <http://mathforum.org/pow/teacher/samples/MathForumSample GeometryPacket.pdf>.
Victoria County History Schools' Learning Zone at <http://www.victoriacountyhistory.ac.uk/ schools/content/teachingmaterial.html>.

Index

Lightning Source UK Ltd.
Milton Keynes UK
UKHW02f1704090818
327005UK00004B/240/P